ADULT LEARNING
ADULT TEACHING

Third Edition

John Daines, Carolyn Daines and Brian Graham

WITHDRAWN

Welsh academic press

Published in Wales by Welsh Academic Press, an imprint of

Ashley Drake Publishing Ltd
PO Box 733
Cardiff
CF14 2YX
www.ashleydrake.com

First published by University of Nottingham, Continuing Education Department 1988
Reprinted 1990, 1991
Second edition published 1992
Reprinted with minor amendments 1993
Third Edition published 1993
Reprinted 1994, 1995, 1996, 1997, 1998

Published by Welsh Academic Press 2002

ISBN   1 86057 078X

British Library Cataloguing-in-Publication Data.
A CIP catalogue for this book is available from the British Library.

Printed by The Lavenham Press, Suffolk.

Contents

IV Reviewing learning

V Getting started

... and ...

Preface

This book is intended to provide some specific and practical suggestions for those involved in teaching and working with adults. It is concerned with the ways that adults learn and how teachers, tutors and trainers can help them learn more efficiently. Much of the book is based upon what we have learned over a number of years of teaching adults and running training courses for adult education tutors, for tutor trainers and for many other professional groups who increasingly find themselves in the business of adult learning and teaching.

This third edition has several new sections and it is produced in a new format. We have tried to provide an accessible and practical account of how to set about the effective planning, preparation and teaching of courses for adults.

The book is in two major parts. The first is concerned with adult learning — adults as learners, their characteristics and expectations. We have included here a section about equal opportunities and access, issues that the reader will also find embedded in our discussion of teaching strategies in the rest of the book. The second part is concerned with adult teaching and is divided into four: planning for learning, teaching methods, reviewing learning (including assessment of competence) and 'getting started'. At the end of the book we have included some titles for further reading and some notes about staff development and training opportunities.

We hope that the ideas and suggestions we have included in this book will both confirm you in what you are already doing well, and help you to reflect upon and develop your practice to the benefit of the adults you work with.

Enjoy your teaching.

John Daines, Carolyn Daines and Brian Graham

ADULT LEARNING

Until recently, it was generally assumed that adults continue to acquire new knowledge and skills in much the same way as they did when they were children. However, as we discover more about how the brain works and investigate more closely what young people and adults actually do, it begins to look as if this view is over-simplistic.

It is not yet possible to say whether adult learning differs qualitatively and quantitatively from that of children in significant ways, though some believe that this is the case. Nevertheless, it does seem that people do have differing preferred learning styles, that they pass through a number of cognitive developmental stages and that some particular aspects of their memory performance may change with increasing age. Whatever the exact nature of the differences, there can be little doubt that, compared to children, adults bring a massive amount of acquired knowledge and experience to new learning situations. They possess considerable practical experience of the process of acquiring knowledge and skills, usually through problem solving, though little of this will have taken place in a classroom or with the help of a professional tutor.

As teachers of adults we need to take full acount of the nature of adult learning. The next few pages consider some of the more important features.

I   Adults as learners

1   Learning in adulthood

It is not appropriate here to describe the psychology of conditioning and learning nor to discuss current 'theories' of adult learning in any detail. What may be of value, however, is to draw some of the key points from our present knowledge of adult learning processes which have implications for teachers of adults.

1   It is not true that once we arrive at biological maturity we reach a mental plateau from which we then begin to deteriorate and the potential for new learning decreases. Given freedom from disease, injury or abuse, the human brain can and does remain fully functioning throughout life. The adage 'you can't teach a dog new tricks' is quite misleading since as people get older they so obviously can and do learn new things.

2   Some physical capabilities do decline with age — sensory acuity; strength; stamina — but it is unlikely that such physiological losses have any significant effect upon learning potential.

3   In practical terms 'learning' may be described both as a process and its outcomes. It involves a change in an individual's knowledge, skills, values or attitudes which lasts over a period of time. The active mental synthesis which takes place may or may not be consciously intended. Expressed in more psychological terms, this cognitive process is made up of three inter-related activities: the original act of learning ('acquisition'), memory ('storage'), and recall or remembering ('retrieval'). From this perspective learning may be taken to be the mechanism by which we gain our impressions of the world and of our place within it, whether the learning is being consciously undertaken through education and/or training or it is occurring 'sub-consciously' throughout day-to-day existence. What is experienced and acquired by the individual — images, sounds, thoughts and emotions — is retained in 'memory' and stored for subsequent use. Remembering is finding or retrieving this data as it is needed.

4 Paradoxically, 'memory' is both reliable and unreliable. For example, we do remember things we see, but what we see is coloured by our physical and emotional perceptions at the time. We also tend to remember things that we are interested in and that are important to us. Fortunately, much of our daily experience is not stored permanently and the irrelevant is either not noticed or memory for it decays rapidly. Moreover, memories can be overlaid with more recent learning; we may forget things because we have a lot of similar information to sift through or we have more significant thoughts competing for our attention. For the elderly, the past may become more important than the mundane present.

5 Learning is more likely to occur where the material is relevant to the individual and/or where it can be linked to what is already known. However, people require time (and sometimes help) to recognise relationships between the new and the already known and to make the appropriate connections.

6 On some occasions new material may conflict with what is already known. Existing opinions and knowledge can 'interfere' with learning, making it more difficult to come to terms with and acquire new ideas, attitudes and behaviour. An individual's current physical state — fatigue, illness, etc — can affect how, what and when s/he learns, though feelings and disposition also play a rather more significant part in overall learning and achievement. Some aspects of people's personalities which have effects upon their learning are anxiety about potential or imagined failure, stress, 'emotional blocks' and lack of self-confidence.

7 Discovering that learning is useful and rewarding results in people being more likely to continue with, return to, or repeat the task. Some learning can be shaped; when an individual receives praise or reward for a partially successful action and information on how to improve performance, s/he will modify the approach and try again to achieve greater success.

2   Characteristics of adult learners

People come to adult education from widely varying backgrounds at different stages of life, each one an individual with his/her own personal strengths, anxieties and hopes. The tutor's job is to recognise the uniqueness of each person and to work in ways that will best help that individual to achieve his/her learning objectives. Nevertheless, there are a number of characteristics which may usefully describe the common features of adult learners.

1   Adults bring to their studies a considerable store of knowledge and experience gained over the years, much of which will be relevant to what is being learnt. They are able to transfer what they already know to their current learning.

2   Adults inevitably bring established attitudes, patterns of thought and fixed ways of doing things to their learning which can help them cope with new situations and ideas. At the same time, over-learnt habits and strongly-held beliefs can be disadvantageous where they prevent individuals from seriously considering something new, whether it is a different technique, an alternative set of values, a recent development or an original idea.

3   Adults can be expected to assume responsibility for themselves. In their everyday lives they are accustomed to setting their own goals and deciding what they want to do and how they want to do it. Thus when they join a group of their own volition they may not respond too well to being told what to do without good reason, especially when they have ideas and plans of their own. (Where an adult is in some way required to attend s/he may actively resent being there at all, let alone be receptive to further direction by a tutor.)

4   Though adults may not have been directly involved in formal education for some years, they will nevertheless have learnt a great deal in the course of their lives since leaving school or college. Their learning may not have been drawn from general principles and theories, nor may it have involved a great deal of abstract thought. They are much more likely to have been handling concrete issues and to have solved practical problems for themselves 'by doing'. Their 'implicit theory' will have been drawn from their practice through trial, error and success.

5   Adults may find it difficult to recall isolated facts and to learn under pressure. On the other hand, they have increased powers of comprehension and of organising material into meaningful 'wholes'.

6   Adults are likely to lack confidence in themselves as learners and to under-estimate their own powers. They tend to be over-anxious and reluctant to risk making mistakes. Above all they will not want to fail or look foolish. These reactions can be particularly prevalent in students who have had poor experiences of learning at school. These negative reactions are also likely to be strongly felt by those who have had lifelong experiences of inequality and prejudice. Any sense of anxiety can be a handicap for adult learners especially where they feel they have to learn in overly-competitive or hostile situations.

7   Adults are unlikely to be satisfied with a time perspective that sees learning as a lengthy process in which the attainment of a desired objective is in the distant future. For many people the value of learning is predominantly immediate rather than long-term. Nevertheless, they recognise that they will not be able to acquire everything straightaway nor necessarily be successful on the first occasion they attempt something. They are likely to be satisfied with a balance: some current success which can be seen to be building into an achievable and satisfying goal later.

8   The learning commitment of adults is normally part-time. They often combine attending a course with family responsibilities and with full-time occupations, whether they work in the home, in paid employment or in an unwaged capacity. They may not be able to devote much additional time to their studies beyond the confines of the course, however interested or motivated they are.

3 Adult expectations

Adults possess clearly defined expectations about their tutors and the courses they attend. Whilst adult student expectations may alter with experience, they need to be taken into account at all stages of the teaching process.

1 Adults expect the tutor to know his/her subject. They do not expect encyclopaedic knowledge and they may well respect a tutor for saying that s/he does not know the answer to a particular question. However, they do expect tutors to demonstrate a firm grasp of the subject material, whether they are giving a formal talk, demonstrating a skill or leading a discussion.

2 Adults expect the tutor to show enthusiasm for the subject and to have a sense of eagerness to teach and to learn from others. They want to see the tutor as a model of good practice, competently demonstrating the skills being learnt and embodying the principles being espoused. In short, adult students expect tutors to practise what they preach.

3 Adults expect the tutor to be a competent teacher and to employ the necessary teaching skills when working with a group. They expect the tutor to have planned and prepared a session well, to be a good communicator, to be able to use a variety of teaching methods and teaching resources and, above all, to manage the overall learning situation effectively.

Ironically, some adults may at first expect to be taught in old-fashioned ways; they will remember being 'talked at' in school and they may anticipate that similar approaches are still in use. Students may initially be rather taken aback by requests to participate actively in the group, to offer their experiences and knowledge, and to take responsibility for their own learning and achievements.

4 Adults expect value for money. They want to attend a course which is pitched at the right level, relevant to their needs and which matches their abilities. The problem is that these features vary from one individual to another, producing what tutors describe as a 'mixed ability' group. Many of the potential difficulties arising from such a group can be solved to most people's satisfaction by a careful

specification of what the course is about, sensitive initial assessment and guidance for individual students, and the use of a variety of methods and approaches during the course.

5 Adults expect to be made to work and to achieve something as a result. Whilst at times they may complain about the effort they have to make, they do not expect it all to be easy. Few adults attend for social reasons alone and it is unlikely they will stay away because realistic demands are made of them.

6 Adults expect to be told how well they are doing as individuals and as members of the group, whether they are studying a practical skill, a creative skill, a physical activity, a language or an intellectual discipline. Feedback to students about their progress should include not only a yardstick of present success but also constructive and positive advice about what they can do to carry on and improve a learning task.

7 Adults expect to enjoy their learning. They are unlikely to give up their time and money where the whole learning experience is dour, unexciting and unenjoyable.

8 Adults expect their adult status to be recognised. Quite properly, they expect to be treated with respect and dignity on a course as elsewhere. They will not put up with harsh criticism, humiliation or being patronised. Ultimately they can choose to vote with their feet if they do not find the equality of adulthood that is their right.

4   Adult motivation

Adults participate in adult education for a variety of reasons. They usually have more than one motive though they may have difficulty in articulating them.

1   Some common motives include:
   - to follow-up an existing interest
   - to learn or develop a skill
   - to learn or develop ideas
   - to create something
   - to satisfy curiosity
   - to save money
   - to discover 'if I can'
   - to gain the approval of others
   - to obtain a qualification
   - to 'access' some further learning opportunity
   - to meet like-minded people
   - to make social contact
   - to gain social self-confidence
   - to enhance self-esteem.

2   The motives people have will in part determine their responses both to the tutor and to the course. Where individuals are highly task-orientated they may not react well to group methods and activities which they perceive as lacking in direct purpose. Those who are interested in greater personal development and social interaction may be happier with a relaxed, informal approach and a more 'democratic' tutor style.

3   For many adults there will be times when their motivation is low and they feel discouraged. Membership of the group may not be as rewarding as first anticipated, parts of the course might be proving too difficult or they might feel that they are not being treated as they had hoped. Some of the disincentives to learning include:
   - failure to achieve
   - lack of overall purpose
   - unrealistic goals
   - an unfriendly atmosphere

- poor class organisation and management
- an uncomfortable environment
- inadequate resources
- little individual attention
- a patronising and/or unfriendly tutor
- poor group support.

4   If students are to maintain an optimum level of learning motivation, they must identify and work to realistic goals that are within their capabilities and then experience some ongoing success in attaining them.

5   It is evident that a tutor's personal style, commitment and enthusiasm are all major motivating factors in helping adult students to continue learning. Students respond to tutors who show genuine interest and concern in individual achievements, who support and encourage them as adult learners, and who interact with them on equal terms.

6   People learn best when:
- they feel secure and they can try out things in safety
- their needs are being met in ways that they can see are relevant and appropriate
- they know what they have to do, especially where they have been involved in setting their own goals
- they are actively involved and engaged
- they know how well they are doing
- they see and experience that they are welcomed and respected both as adults and as individuals in their own right.

5   Adult learners: equal opportunities and access

Equal opportunities has to do with ensuring that everyone, whatever his/her life circumstances, has a right to appropriate and accessible education and training. Many people — especially women, the elderly, the less affluent, members of ethnic-minority communities, people with disabilities, those who are educationally disadvantaged — have missed out on educational opportunities during their lives. The adult education sector is not blameless in restricting people's access to provision, though efforts are now being made to remove institutional barriers and to make access much easier.

This is not the place to examine the nature of prejudice or the origins of inequality and how they adversely affect so many people. Suffice it to say that inequality continues to exist even with the law as it is. Teachers of adults, whatever their subjects, have a part to play in helping to break down inequality and promoting continuing education for all.

1   Consider your own attitudes and knowledge about the variety of people you teach. The expectations you have, the way you behave and the language you use may all say something about you, the way you perceive people in general and your students in particular. You may be aware, and so may they, that you respond differently to those of a markedly different age, to men or women, to those with some form of disability and/or educational disadvantage, to those from a different racial, ethnic and/or cultural background, to those of different sexual orientation. You have a professional duty to behave in ways acceptable to all, and this means accepting every adult student as of equal worth irrespective of race, gender, ability, background, or disposition.

2   As a representative of the institution or agency which employs you, you should ensure that everything is being done at the organisational level to ensure access. You should obtain a copy of the institution's equal opportunities policy document: read it and continually monitor that what it says is being put into practice. Amongst other things, you could check out how courses are being publicised and in what languages; the overall way that course timings coincide with public transport, school hours and holidays; the arrangements for the elderly and people with disabilities; the provision of crèche and playgroup facilities, the flexibility of enrolment procedures; the fee arrangements for the unwaged and those on low incomes, and so on.

3 You need to think through the ways in which you, as teacher, offer your subject. If you normally teach a course made up of a sequence of weekly sessions, you could think what other formats might be possible that would increase access to potential students eg taster sessions, weekend day schools, a 'roll-on-roll-off' course, evenings instead of day or *vice versa*, a course in an outreach centre or local hall, a group for 'women only'. Ask your students for their opinions. If you change the emphasis or style of your course publicity 'blurb', it may attract a wider range of potential students by making it clear that you are keen to work with a diversity of people.

4 The way you organise your teaching group should take into account any special needs your students may have. Those who have a hearing or visual impairment should be offered an optimum position near the front. Discuss with these students what aids might be employed to assist their learning. Those with physical disabilities should have appropriate space and seating whilst those who attend with personal helpers should be accommodated in ways which they feel best suit their particular need. As tutor, you have a responsibility for discovering in sensitive ways how you, the group and the institution can best aid your student colleagues in the pursuance of their learning objectives.

5 There are several 'extra-classroom' features that you should also give thought to — the availability and use of refreshment facilities, comfortable sitting areas, cloakrooms, library and resource centre, etc, and the access that your students have to them socially and physically. You have a responsibility to see that your students' personal needs as well as their educational needs are catered for.

6 Trying to provide all of your students with access to your subject matter and helping them achieve some personal success will not be easy. There is no magic formula. You must undertake a continuous process of reflection and analysis of what you do and how you do it to ensure that you are giving everyone a chance to engage with your subject with as few barriers as possible. Amongst other things:

  * Take care that the language and references you or your students use do not offend. Avoid using terms that have negative overtones of race, gender, culture, sexual orientation, age or disability; find and use more acceptable words and phrases.

* The examples and images that you offer, whether in speech, visual displays or in written materials should reflect and acknowledge the diversity of people and of their experience. Ensure as far as you can that the examples and experiences that you elicit and value from your students also reflect this diversity. If they are consistently restricted or mono-cultural, provide some additions of your own to extend people's awareness of the reality around them.

* The expectations that you have of students and of their potential and actual achievements should relate to them as individuals and not as members of a particular community. You may need to help individuals recognise and surmount the personal barriers they experience — " because I am a woman ... black ... hard of hearing ... suffering from the after-effects of a stroke ... ". You must act in accord with the belief that change and development is possible for all, regardless of people's life circumstances and that your function is to do what you can to assist this process for all your students.

KEY POINTS

❏ **Adults are likely to learn more effectively when the learning tasks are seen to be relevant, meaningful, interesting and useful.**

❏ **Adults have wide experience and knowledge of the world yet they often lack confidence in themselves as learners.**

❏ **Adults expect to be treated with the respect and the equality of adulthood.**

❏ **The motives people have for attending may vary but achieving some success will increase their motivation for further learning.**

❏ **You should demonstrate your commitment to equal opportunities through everything you say and do in your work with adult students.**

ADULT TEACHING

When people are asked what makes for a good adult course (or session) they invariably identify the same sorts of factors. Their views can be categorised into three major groups:

The first has to do with course design. People describe a 'good' course as being relevant to their needs with clear statements of purpose and having appropriate content presented at the right level and pace. In addition, they value a variety of interesting teaching and learning methods, together with opportunities to try out what they have learnt with feedback about how they are doing. The second category might be called 'principles, values and tutor style'. What is of importance to people is that as participants they are treated in adult ways, their experience is welcomed and valued, they actively participate, and that they feel at ease with each other and with what is taking place within the group. They think that tutors need to be enthusiastic and enjoy what they do, sensitive to the needs of both individuals and the group, professionally competent as teachers and subject specialists, and good communicators willing to share as equals in the life of the group. Finally, people itemise a whole range of factors which have to do with efficient organisation and administration. These include domestic issues such as physical access, refreshments, seating, a clean and comfortable environment, as well as adequate pre-course communication and subsequent follow-up. They also judge that the quality of a course is demonstrated by its marketing and publicity, the quality of the materials, time-keeping and attention to detail.

In summary, adults say that a good course or session is one that helps them to engage in relevant learning experiences in a variety of interesting ways with the help of a responsive and supportive tutor. Above all, a good course is one that respects their adulthood. The rest of this book is about how we, as tutors, can respond to these quite reasonable expectations of the people we work with.

II Planning for learning

Introduction

It is evident to any teacher of adults that actual face-to-face work is only part of the business of teaching. Planning and preparation are as necessary prerequisites for a teaching/learning event as are assessment and evaluation after it. There are no short cuts in this process. As a tutor you will need to determine what it is that people want and for what purposes. From such analyses, in which the opinions of adult students themselves play an important part, you will be able to identify what you need to teach, what methods to employ and what equipment and resources to use. Reflection upon what took place will indicate what students actually achieved and the ways in which the session could be improved another time. It should also provide clear indications as to what should be done on the next occasion the group meets.

The elements of preparation and planning for teaching can be represented in a simple diagram; the following pages deal with each element in turn.

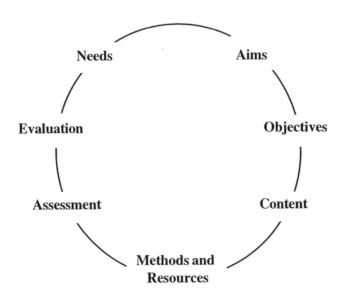

6   Needs

Planning for learning starts at the point of needs analysis: what is it that the intended learners need at their particular levels of development within a subject area? Once known, this information will help determine the appropriate concepts, knowledge, procedures and skills with which they should engage. Where a subject has a representative body or is part of a national curriculum there will probably be a hierarchical system of qualifications and assessment procedures, supported by clearly defined syllabuses and course guidelines. Such material can prove invaluable to the tutor, representing as it does the combined wisdom of recognised experts and teachers within the field. However, it cannot take into account the particular needs, expectations and aspirations of every individual who might join an adult group. Thus, even where tutors have the benefit of published curriculum guidelines, they need to find out about the specific needs of their adult students and use this knowledge to assist in their planning.

1   There are a number of ways by which you might identify the needs of the particular group of adults you are to work with. You could:

   – talk with other experienced teachers of your subject and find out what they have done with groups at similar levels
   – attend the enrolment session and talk with potential students. Ask them what they hope to gain from the course and what expectations they have of themselves, of the course and of you the tutor
   – write to enrolled students before the course commences and ask them about their expectations and hopes for the course. You could include a draft syllabus and ask them to comment and make suggestions for additional topics
   – hold an informal pre-course meeting and seek to identify their expectations in a similar way
   – run an informal pre-course meeting, taster session or a one-day school and build a section into it when participants are asked to give their opinions, preferences and expectations for the subsequent course
   – make contact with previous students and ask for their judgments: *On reflection, what would you have found most useful, helpful, enjoyable ... ?*

2 Whilst some of these procedures can undoubtedly help you, you will, in the end, have to rely on your own experience as a subject specialist and teacher as to the most appropriate design for a course at a particular level. You will have to determine the overall structure and work out how and when to tackle each section. You would be advised, however, to restrict your detailed session planning to the first few sessions, since the experience and feedback you gain from these early meetings with the group will assist your planning and execution of later ones.

KEY POINTS

❑ **Find out what your intending students hope to gain from the course.**

❑ **Trust your judgment but be prepared to modify what you decide in the light of what happens.**

---

7   Aims and objectives

A great deal has been written about aims and objectives in education though fortunately most of it need not concern us here. However, in planning any learning event thought does need to be given to these two aspects as they are the means by which what is to be attempted and what students are to achieve are specified. Unless tutor and students are clear about what they are trying to do, they won't know how to set about doing it, let alone be in a position to decide whether they have attained anything worthwhile at the end.

Aims are general statements representing ideals or aspirations; they are statements of intent. They are used to indicate the overall purpose of a course or programme. When written rather more specifically, they can also serve to describe the purpose of an individual session. However carefully aims are written, they do not say what participants will actually be learning and achieving at specific points. The down to earth, concrete statements which identify such things are known as objectives.

1   **Aims** describe the overall purpose(s) of a complete learning sequence. They are usually long-term, difficult to evaluate and expressed in rather general terms such as:

   – to improve understanding, general skills or physical co-ordination
   – to modify attitudes, beliefs or standards
   – to impart information, knowledge or ideas
   – to stimulate action
   – to encourage changes in behaviour.

   Aims say what a course hopes to achieve: *This course will help participants to understand ... to achieve... to respond to...* something or other. In the context of a course about road safety for cyclists, for example, the course aim could be: *To increase the personal safety and cycling skills of course participants, and to promote their awareness of, and their reactions to the behaviour of other road users.* Course aims are broad brush strokes, they do not give details.

2   A general statement is also needed at the next level of description, setting out the overall purpose of each individual session. Since it describes one session rather than a whole course it needs to be written more specifically.

Some teachers use the same type of language for session aims as they use for course aims. Using the cycling example again, a session aim might be: *To improve the recognition of the more dangerous cycling manoeuvres and to develop appropriate safety strategies.* Other teachers prefer to express the purpose of a session by stating it in terms of general student outcomes — what participants will achieve. In the cycling example: *Participants will be able to recognise the more dangerous cycling manoeuvres and to develop appropriate safety strategies.*

The difference between the two is as much one of language as anything else. In effect they both describe overall purpose and, by implication at least, what it is hoped participants will work towards. Different authors use different terminology — statement of purpose, session goals, session aims, teaching objectives, general objectives. However, as long as you end up with a clearly expressed statement of what the session is about which has meaning for you and helps direct your planning, you should express it in the way that suits you best.

3 **Objectives** are specific action statements. They are achievable stepping stones which lead towards more generally expressed aims. They are the most specific level of description used and they state in some detail the hoped-for changes in the learner. Objectives say what the student will be able to do or think or feel or say as a result of the planned learning/teaching event. They are typically expressed using 'action' verbs such as:

– identify	– state	– choose
– select	– move	– participate
– criticise	– perform	– compare
– show	– conclude	– demonstrate

and they need to be written in ways that allow the teacher and the student to make some judgment as to whether or not they have been achieved.

In the example of a cycling safety session, one objective might be: *The student will be able to mount his/her bicycle from the kerbside and check for oncoming traffic without falling off.* Another might be: *The student will be able to demonstrate the hand signals for left turn, right turn and straight on correctly to an observer positioned in front.* A third might be: *The student will be able to explain the safety requirements for front and rear lights and for reflectors as specified in the Highway Code.*

4   Objectives are said to have 3 functions:

  – they provide an overall structure for a learning/teaching event
  – they help in detailed planning
  – they act as a basis for appropriate assessment procedures.

Thus, as far as possible, objectives should not only describe the desired behaviour but also the conditions under which attainment is to be demonstrated, and the criteria for such success. However, some changes in behaviour may not be observable until some time after a session has finished.

5   Objectives are also given various names by different writers — behavioural objectives, learning objectives, instructional objectives, teaching objectives — but again, the way they are labelled is much less critical than their function. The crucial point is that you think out exactly what your students are to achieve by the end of a session. You should use behavioural terms and ensure that the statements you come up with are specific, limited in scope, attainable and observable. Once you are clear what they are, you can then set about planning the session — selecting the content, choosing the best methods, gathering the resources together, working out how to monitor outcomes.

6   Not every learning outcome in a particular session may, in fact, be planned for. In the example of cycling safety it may be that as a result of a session, some car-driving students become much more aware of the sense of danger and physical exposure experienced by people who ride bicycles. They may respond subsequently in much more courteous ways to the cyclists they encounter on the road. Some teachers describe these unanticipated results as 'windfall outcomes'.

As a tutor you could also remain quite unaware of some of the more personal, expressive objectives that individuals may achieve, though these may be highly significant to them. As a result of a newly-acquired sense of freedom as a more confident cyclist for example, a student may enjoy a more personal and 'meaningful' contact with nature and the countryside. You can but hope that all your students achieve similar outcomes of personal value beyond those you plan for them in your sessions.

7 However you decide to write down your intended purposes for each session, you need at some point to think about what it is you want your students to be able to do, or think, or say by the end that they could not do before. Some of the objectives you have in mind may well remain the same over several sessions, but until you identify what it is you want students to achieve you will be ill-equipped to plan a session, teach it or discover whether it was successful. Time spent thinking out your aims and objectives, and talking them through with your group will pay handsome dividends in terms of your planning and teaching, their learning and achievement, and your mutual feelings of success.

KEY POINTS

❑ **Specify aims in understandable language that will tell people whether or not the course is for them.**

❑ **Clarify objectives by using the phrase ' by the end of the session students will be able to ...' Avoid words such as 'know', 'understand', 'appreciate' etc.**

---

8   Content

Deciding what the subject content should be for a particular session appears at first sight to be relatively straightforward. Tutors are generally well-versed in their subjects and whilst they may not be experts in all aspects they will know where to go for necessary information. Similarly, most will have acquired the crucial skills within their particular area and though their own performance might not be perfect every time, they know how the activity should be carried out. Yet knowing one's subject does not always make the selection and structuring of content easy.

Whilst it would be unrealistic to attempt to write specific guidelines for the scores of different subjects taught to adults, here are some general suggestions that may be of help to you.

1   You should be quite clear in your own mind about the purpose and scope of a course before you start trying to select any of the detailed content you might teach. First, think about the course in general terms ('aims') and come up with a working title that sounds attractive and unambiguous. When you have a rough idea what the course is going to be about, think it through in more precise terms, including what you hope people will be able to do or think or feel or say by the end ('objectives'). Now identify the intermediate steps they will have to take to get there — what will they have to know or be able to do at each stage of the course so that they can move on to the next? By coming up with a series of statements in a 'hierarchy' — if this, then that — you will begin to construct a course outline. To 'flesh it out' with potential subject content ask yourself: *What exactly will they have to know at this point in order to achieve x... what content will they have to learn about that they won't already know ... and so which aspects will I need to include and teach?* You will by now have the basis of a course structure and an indication of the necessary content for individual sessions.

2   It may help you to reflect on the conceptual framework of your subject — what are the fundamental tenets and skills on which it rests? Rethinking your subject from an adult learner's view point can help your own understanding of it and help you determine which sections of it you might teach. Many tutors are prisoners of their subject traditions and their own training within them. You should not expect to guide people through every avenue, but you can provide them with

the important principles and skills that they need at their particular stage of development and which they will then be able to transfer to new situations.

This does not mean that you must teach everything from first principles. It will probably be more appropriate, especially at the start, for you to provide students with sufficient critical points that will enable them to move on. (They do not need to know global warming theory to judge whether it will rain tomorrow!) Because they are adults with knowledge, experience and expertise in other content areas, they will understand what you are doing if you share your strategy with them. They know that they do not need to understand everything about a subject to deal with the issue that is of interest to them at that moment. Draw any theory from practice and experience rather than the other way round.

3   Once you have a clear idea of what you might include, err on the side of less content rather than more. Whilst it is probably quite a good idea to prepare more material than you think you might need for a particular session, resist the temptation to teach more than is absolutely necessary. The most common mistake tutors make is to cram in too much content. It is much more rewarding for students to be able to use some of the important knowledge and skills of your subject rather than be exposed to yet more material which they cannot possibly absorb. Most of us seem to have an unstoppable desire to tell people everything we know. It is as if our enthusiasm for our subject, coupled with a feeling of guilt about short-changing students, stops us from recognising the principles of good adult learning and teaching.

4   You may be working to an external syllabus and feel that you are compelled to teach all the content it specifies. If you find out what your students already know and what they feel they need, you should be able to select what material is essential, what is peripheral and what they already know sufficiently well for you to be able to move on. Syllabuses rarely indicate the structure and emphases to be placed on particular topics nor do they usually specify the approach which should be taken. You are quite at liberty to decide, in consultation with your group, how a topic is to be tackled. There is probably much greater freedom to select and prioritise the content defined by a syllabus than would at first appear. Syllabuses are as much guides as directives.

5 Many of the same points can be made about books, especially those which you may have selected as course texts. They are a learning resource rather than a teaching prescription. Even where you are using a commercial learning package — such as the sort the BBC produces for languages — you should select, re-order, emphasise and extend as seems best to you to meet the particular needs of the individuals you are working with.

6 Not all the subject content that you think your students should engage with has to be presented during a session. Some of it will certainly lend itself to self-study or individual practice. Adults are responsible to themselves for their own learning, though they share with you the responsibility for the course. Thus you are at liberty to negotiate with them the areas of content that they might follow up on their own rather than in session time. You will have to guide such 'distance learning' and help them decide whether their private study can best be under-taken through the use of handouts, a reading plan or a practice schedule. However, ensure you resist the temptation of packing the spaces you create in your sessions with yet more content!

7 The subject content for a session does not have to be 'for all the people, all of the time'. Most groups consist of individuals with differing experiences, levels of expertise and potential for learning. More advanced students will be able to work with subject content that is not appropriate for beginners in the group. One of the advantages of organising participants into sub-groups is that you can choose the material each group is to work with to match their needs more exactly.

8 You should also watch out for the occasions when several students have much the same needs at a particular time. This can often happen in practical subjects where people are working on their own projects. Gathering an *ad hoc* group together will allow you to present some new content to them more efficiently, be it a new technique or an additional piece of knowledge. In so doing, you may be satisfying those who cannot proceed any further without it and preparing those who are beginning to reach the stage where they need it. Moreover, by specifically targeting a piece of content to a particular sub-group you will not interrupt other members of the group who would not benefit from it at that moment.

9 Many tutors lack confidence in their own knowledge and expertise. Some spend hours studying everything they can put their hands on in a desperate attempt both to fill supposed gaps in their knowledge and to find the ultimate answer of what to teach to others. Keep up-to-date in your subject by all means, indeed you have a professional duty to do so, but focus less upon what you feel you do not know and more upon what your students need you to teach them.

KEY POINTS

❑ **Use the test 'need to know — nice to know' when deciding on what content to include.**

❑ **Prepare sufficient content, but if you teach less of it they may learn rather more.**

---

9 Consultation and negotiation

There is much to be said for involving adult students in decision-making processes within adult education settings, not least because it is a clear recognition of their equality and adulthood. Within the context of a course, discussion between the group members and the tutor about such things as the aims and objectives of a course and the way it is planned and organised, the subject content, the learning/teaching methods to be used and the manner in which the students and the course are to be evaluated, demonstrates a commitment to the notion of student responsibility for, and 'ownership' of their own learning. Experience indicates that the opportunity to share in the making of decisions about a course increases student interest, commitment, motivation and learning.

Two distinct processes are involved, either separately or in tandem. In the first, consultation, the tutor consults the group but retains the option of whether or not to modify his/her proposals. In the second, negotiation, the decision to adopt a particular direction or to make a change is a mutual one, agreed by the group and tutor together. The different opinions that tutors hold about the use of consultation and negotiation with their adult groups in part reflect their individual beliefs about the nature of the tutor-student relationship and the implicit contract of a course description. Their attitudes may also be influenced by judgments of the likely level of prior subject knowledge and of the adult educational experience of a particular group.

1 All consultation and negotiation take place within given parameters, eg institutional regulations, timing and environmental constraints, the availability of resources, syllabus and/or examination requirements, as well as the inherent demands of the subject discipline and the tutor's capabilities. Certain aspects of a course or session may simply not be 'up for grabs' and in such instances you can only relay the relevant information with appropriate explanation and rationale. However, it ought to be possible for you to strike a realistic balance between those aspects of the course which are for 'information only', those for 'consultation' and those which are 'negotiable'.

2 Negotiation, unlike consultation, demands some level of knowledge on the part of group members. It cannot be undertaken from a position of ignorance. Group participants must possess an optimum level of

awareness of the issues involved and of the subject under consideration if they are going to share in such decisions.They must also be
aware of the consequences of a particular decision, ie if **A** is chosen,
then **B** may have to be forfeited.

3   The process of negotiation, and to some extent consultation, is likely
to prove strange to many adult students and upsetting to some. It is not
likely to have been a feature of their previous education and some may
still see the tutor as 'expert'. Where this is likely to be the case, you
need to introduce negotiation with care: too much, too soon will be
counter-productive.

4   It is incumbent upon you to initiate some procedure whereby a group
is empowered to undertake negotiation of some (or all) of the curriculum and of the course's (or session's) organisation and management.
This may be done in a number of ways, including the following:

*   Where your group is unfamiliar with the concept of negotiation or
    does not possess the knowledge to make a valid contribution to a
    discussion, you could commence by consulting them about most
    issues whilst beginning the process of negotiation of a few. You
    could select some of the more practical issues such as starting on
    time, homework, smoking and coffee breaks and ask people to
    agree some ground rules. As the course progresses, you can suggest
    they might like to negotiate about other aspects too.

*   You could prepare and run a preliminary sequence of activities at
    the start of the course which will help group participants recognise
    their existing knowledge as well as lead them to identify their own
    needs. Such a procedure carried out during the first (and perhaps
    second) session will provide them with an optimum level of
    knowledge to engage in negotiation and take informed decisions
    with you about what is to be done during the rest of the course.

*   Where you judge people already possess the appropriate knowl-
    edge on which to base their judgments, you could contact them
    before the course takes place and ask them to propose in writing the
    topics (and procedures) they would like to see included. You take
    the responsibility for producing an overall structure based on the
    strength of demand, presenting it to them for their confirmation
    when you meet in the first session.

    *   Where a group can engage in total negotiation from the outset and would want to do so face to face, you can devote the first part of the course to the process. This is the least plannable of all procedures and it can take an inordinate amount of time as well lead to periods of intense frustration. Nevertheless, the outcomes in terms of shared responsibility and commitment to both individual and group learning can considerable.

5   Some potentially negotiable areas include:

    – content of the course
    – order and structure of the subject content
    – ways of teaching and learning
    – assignments/student work
    – assessment and evaluation
    – attendance
    – the environment (venue, classroom layout, smoking)
    – times and timing (start/finish, coffee breaks etc)
    – resources and materials (supply and cost)
    – social activities.

It may be that neither you nor the group has the power to enact a desired change or modification. In such circumstances, you can carry on the process of negotiation on behalf of the group with those who have such power, ie institutional managers or those with responsibility for the subject and its standards.

6   Whatever level of negotiation procedure you use, it is crucial that you monitor the discussion carefully and try to keep the emotional temperature down. You should provide guidance and advice, pointing out the potential results of a particular proposal whilst indicating aspects or topics that may have been ignored or inappropriately discarded. You should keep the group in touch with accepted procedures and subject rationale as well as making your own contribution about what you believe might or might not be included. The group will want to know your preferences and hear what you think about their proposals.

7   Negotiation carries with it shared responsibility for its results. The group must recognise that decisions may not necessarily benefit them in the ways they intended or foresaw. At the end of the discussions, you should summarise what has been proposed, making sure that everyone understands the implications of what they are agreeing to; you should then set about implementing the decisions.

8 If all this talk about negotiation frightens you, reflect for a moment. The chances are that you are already doing it with your adult students though they (and you) may call it *setting ground rules, agreeing what we'll do next time, discussing our next move* or something similar. So it might not be so novel after all.

KEY POINTS

❑ **Share some of the responsibility for the course with students; they will be more committed to making it work as a result.**

❑ **Involve students in making decisions about the course right from the start.**

III   Teaching methods

Introduction

No one method of teaching adults will suit every occasion. What matters is to choose a method or methods which best help adults achieve the task in hand. Experience indicates that a combination of methods is likely to be more effective than any one used singly and that a variety will help maintain people's interest and motivation.

An imaginative choice of teaching methods and their efficient implementation and management will allow students to participate in a range of appropriate activities — listening, looking, talking, doing — and this will facilitate their learning.

1   One way of categorising methods which may help you with their selection is by the type of activity involved:

- **presentation**, where the tutor predominantly transmits ideas, information or skills, for example by lecturing and demonstrating, often using a chalkboard, flip chart, etc
- **interaction**, where knowledge and experience are shared between the teacher and the learners and/or amongst the learners themselves, for example by discussion, questioning, role play and brainstorming
- **search**, where the learners explore and discover for themselves, either on their own or in small collaborative groups, for example by individual practice, problem solving tasks and case studies.

This is potentially a more useful description than the overly-simplistic categories of 'learner centred' and 'teacher centred' which have been in vogue recently. These latter terms, even where they are recognised as being the ends of a continuum, often carry with them an implicit assumption that the former is in some way philosophically and psychologically superior to the latter.

Another bipolar categorisation, that of 'class teaching' and 'circular tour', is at least not value-laden though in truth it only serves to describe the teacher's role.

2   A further way of categorising methods is by 'domains of learning':

 – the **affective domain** is concerned with attitudes. The methods which would be included here are discussion, case study, role play and simulation ...
 – the **psycho motor domain** is concerned with skills. The methods which would be included here are demonstration, individual practice, and coaching ...
 – the **cognitive domain** is concerned with knowledge. The methods which would be included here are lectures, small group work and problem solving tasks ...

3   However, neither of these categorisations provides a fully adequate description. A particular method may be described both as interactive or search and another might as easily facilitate the acquisition of a skill as an item of knowledge. A more complete framework within which to make choices about methods is to think through the question: *which method or methods will best help my students to learn?* whilst bearing in mind:

 – the specific learning objective(s)
 – the type of material
 – the need for variety of activity
 – the methods with which the group is already familiar
 – the group's preferences
 – your familiarity with and liking for the method
 – your skills and ability to manage the method
 – the facilities available.

4   You could choose from:

Lecture/talk *
Lecture/talk with group participation*
Demonstration — showing*
Demonstration — do it with me*
Panel/debate

Discussion*
Small group tasks and activities*
Brainstorming
Buzz group
Visits and field trips

Case study
Role play
Simulation
Games
Seminars

Individual practice and supervision*
Tutorials
Individual projects
Diary
Work between sessions

The following chapters consider each of these methods. The more common (*) are presented in detail whilst the rest are set out in tabular form, showing some of their main features and advantages.

10   Talks, lectures and presentations

There is a view held by some adult educators that the presentation of knowledge in a talk or lecture is in some way improper and demeans those who listen. This denies reality since we all can and do learn effectively from such presentations when they are properly prepared, managed and delivered.

Talks and lectures are an efficient way of providing information and ideas within a specific period of time. Speakers can organise and structure the knowledge they possess and offer it to others with a sense of immediacy. They can develop an argument, outline a field of knowledge, summarise a topic, pose pertinent questions and highlight relevant issues for the benefit of their listeners. Given that people stay mentally active, involved and interested, a talk or lecture can be a quick and effective method of transmission from one person to a number of others.

1   How much material people are able to retain as a result of a sustained period of listening to another depends on a number of features, not least of which are their personal levels of interest and motivation. Some of the important characteristics of good presentations are:

   – clarity
   – logical organisation
   – interest
   – emphasis of important points
   – correct pitch
   – statements to link key points
   – relevance
   – involvement of listeners
   – appropriate examples
   – appropriate resources and AVA

   all of which need to be offered by well prepared and enthusiastic presenters who acknowledge the adulthood of their audiences.

2   Even the most attentive listener may mentally wander off into a 'micro-sleep'. It seems that people's attention often strays after 20 minutes or so of sustained listening. However, those who are given the opportunity to actively manipulate the ideas and information being presented to them — who think about the point just made, recognise

the example being given, extract the principle, examine the relationship between the new and what they already know — are much more likely to learn and remember what they hear than are those who sit passively letting the words wash over them.

3 Learning is something that learners must do for themselves; it is not something that you as teacher can do for them. The way you present your material, however, can have a significant impact on the effectiveness of that learning. It follows that the job of giving a talk calls for careful preparation and skill. You must aim for clarity and interest both in the way you structure your material and the manner in which you deliver it. If you are unintelligible and boring with complex and esoteric content, you cannot expect people to listen, let alone learn.

4 Though there are a number of ways that a talk or lecture can be structured — the 'classical' survey, the sequential description, the problem-centred approach — each can use the same straightforward approach: an orientation, a set of key points and a summary.

* Your opening or **orientation** should gain and hold attention from the start. You need to motivate the listeners as well as inform them, so devise a 'lead-in' which will both capture their interest and be relevant to what you want to talk about. Some tutors begin with an unambiguous statement of the question or problem under discussion. Alternatively, you could start with:

   – a reference to or a request for the listeners' experiences
   – a question ... actual or rhetorical
   – a relevant anecdote
   – a novel object, item, or picture
   – a reference to yourself.

* The **key points** are the important points that make up your exposition. Explain each in turn, avoiding technical terms and complex sentences. Use examples or illustrations that are lucid, unambiguous and recognisable to your listeners.

There are four tactics or verbal markers which you can use which will help people follow what you say. What they are called is not particularly important, but what each one does is! They are:

   – **signposts** which indicate structure and direction. *I'd like to talk about dietary fibre. First, I want to outline what it is; second, to identify* *where it occurs in our foodstuffs; third, to examine the ways in which it is of benefit to us.*

- **frames** which indicate the beginning and end of a sub-topic. *So those are the main characters in the novel. Let's now look at how they first meet each other.*

- **foci** which highlight or emphasise the key points. *So the main point is to measure very accurately and maintain a log of your readings.*

- **links** which join one part of an explanation with another. *So you can see that the French had quite a different concept of colonialism. This begins to explain their reactions to ...*

* The **summary** is a restatement of the important key points. You should not introduce new ideas at this stage though you may use other words to review what you have already said. The way that you link the key points together should lead to your conclusion, the answer to the problem or question you posed at the outset. *To sum up then, let's just look at the main points we've talked about ...*

5 One of the difficulties faced by many tutors is knowing how much to tell people. As was pointed out in Chapter 8 (*Content*), most of us end up telling them too much. So rethink your topic from their point of view and make sure that you tell your listeners only what they need to know 'now'.

* New material should relate in some way to what listeners already know. It is much easier to understand and learn something new about an area that is already familiar than to tackle a topic which is quite novel, and which has no connection to existing knowledge. Where the topic *is* new, you will need to draw analogies and examples that will form bridges between what is already known and what is not.

* Think out your examples and illustrations carefully before you begin: do not hope that they will come to you on the spur of the moment. People like to hear about things from areas with which they are familiar so use concrete examples that relate to their existing experience. The more telling and meaningful your illustration, the more likely people are to remember the ideas to which they relate.

* Check that your listeners comprehend what you are talking about. Look at members of the group and watch for clues and cues of their interest, involvement and attitudes. Ask them if they understand, though you may get a more candid answer if you ask more obliquely: *Are you happy so far or should I go over the main points? I know that one or two are a bit difficult* or something similar. Change your approach or modify what you intend to do if the feedback from your audience warrants it.

6   People do find it difficult to concentrate for long periods of time. Therefore introduce some change of activity. Use buzz groups amongst neighbours and/or give people a simple problem to work out, perhaps checking their answer with a partner. Certainly give everyone a brief break to stretch and to change their sitting positions each half-an-hour or so.

7   Constantly use the experience of your listeners. Asking people to indicate a personal response to a point by a show of hands is a minimal way of doing this. Asking for individual contributions, questions, answers and observations from members of the group involves them more actively, though to start with they may find it a bit of a risk in front of everyone else. (Tell them to think about a point with a partner first and then ask for a combined view, thereby allowing them to share any feeling of exposure).

8   Do not give everything away. It is worth encouraging people to draw their own conclusions and come up with the principles involved rather than always telling them. Pose a question and give them time to think. Encourage them to try out their idea on a partner ... ask if anyone would like to offer you a solution. If they have to struggle a bit mentally, that is no bad thing.

9   Some important communication skills for giving talks and lectures include the following.

   *   Speak clearly and directly to people. This does not mean you have to develop a new voice or different accent. Talk naturally at a pace to suit your listeners. Use pauses and silences as well as altering the tone and pitch of your voice to emphasise what you say.

   *   Effective presentation is about open communication. Look directly at people and meet their eyes. Try not to fix your gaze on the ceiling, your notes, or the clock!

* Movement can help sustain people's attention. Make use of the space between yourself and the group. Avoid becoming frozen to the same spot but do not undertake marathon walks either.

* Most gestures are quite acceptable and help underline what you say. Your personal mannerisms are part of you and unless they are gross they will not be of great consequence to your listeners.

* Avoid using language which is not comprehensible to your students. However, there is no reason why you should not introduce new terminology if you explain it carefully, perhaps noting the terms on board. Jargon is a problem only if people do not understand it.

* Make full use of resources and audio-visual aids to illustrate and enhance your talk and your listeners' understanding.

10 There is a tradition of question time at the end of a talk. If you have a relatively small group this can work quite well, but with a larger audience it can often be stilted and unsatisfactory. One solution is to give people a little time to identify any questions they may have with a partner first. The partner may actually be able to answer the question though it will also give the questioner time to refine his or her question after being reassured that it is a worthwhile one. You could encourage people to ask questions during your talk though it can happen that you are due to cover the substance of a question in the next section!

11 The suggestions given so far refer to a talk or lecture where the level of active group participation is minimal. Such passivity might be appropriate because of the size of the audience, constraints of time or content, or where you judge that a period of quiet listening and reflection is called for. However, when you have the freedom, consider reversing the more normal procedure. Start with a short period of some group interaction — questions, a buzz group, small group work or a practical task — you can then draw upon their observations and tentative solutions in your subsequent discourse. Better still, construct a sequence where your input is interspersed with individual and group activities. A number of variations are possible but some examples are:

    A   Tutor talk
           Buzz group
           Tutor talk
           Comment on slides/pictures
           Tutor talk

B Group activity
Brain storm
Tutor talk
Individual task
Small group comparison
Tutor talk

C Introduction
Video
Review of video
Tutor talk
Small group analysis
Plenary feedback

In each instance the tutor's presentation holds the subsidiary activities together, all of which can quite easily be run even in a lecture theatre with the audience remaining seated. (See *Chapter 25: Working with large groups.)*

12 The lecture/talk with group participation just described allows listeners to contribute and participate more, to experience a greater variety of opinion and information and to interact with others and clarify their own ideas. However you choose to structure your talk or lecture, remember that people respond to speakers who are warm, enthusiastic and stimulating. So smile and try to look as if you enjoy both your subject and the opportunity of sharing it with others.

KEY POINTS

❑ **Challenge people to choose, judge and manipulate ideas rather than leaving them to sit and listen passively.**

❑ **Build some participative activities into your presentation as well as using well-prepared teaching resources and visual aids.**

11   Demonstration

Practical activities in particular require that students receive careful instruction followed by opportunities for guided practice. Common sense says that people learn best from a combination of seeing, hearing and doing. Thus a demonstration, whether of the 'watch me first' variety or the 'do it with me' type should:

- state the activity involved and indicate its purpose and/or outcome
- arouse and maintain students' interest
- reveal the main steps of the activity and identify the likely problem areas
- inspire confidence in students so that they will be willing to try themselves
- be so timed that students can undertake individual practice afterwards and receive feedback about their performance.

1   Before undertaking a demonstration you will need to be clear in your own mind what you are going to demonstrate, and why, and that you yourself can do it adequately.

   *   Break it down into its basic steps or movements. Remember that what is easy and quite comprehensible to you will probably not be to your students. Strive to simplify it. An overslick demonstration may rob people of their self-confidence when they come to do it. You are trying to show them how, not give a royal command performance.

   *   Prepare any teaching aids that will help students understand what is involved. Diagrams and models may well be helpful in addition to anything you may physically be able to show them. The *'Blue Peter'* ... *here's one I've already done* has much to recommend it. Letting your students see one or more examples of the aimed-for finished product at the start will help them put the separate pieces into a meaningful mental whole. Be ready to demonstrate the whole activity to them at the outset.

2   Before starting the demonstration you should describe what you intend to do and why.

   *   Make sure everyone can see as well as hear you. There is nothing wrong with a raised position — a dais, stage or table — if you feel

comfortable there and the students can see you better. Depending upon what you are demonstrating, you could change your position in the room at some point so that you are nearer those at the back. Speak clearly and distinctly, and make eye contact with people.

* 'Show and tell' the finished product. Then run through the main stages of the complete activity so that they know what they are aiming to do. If you can only do the thing once — you have only one set of ingredients or materials — briefly describe the major steps you are going to take, miming the crucial actions or holding up the important components.

3 Begin the demonstration, accompanying each step of your activity with a verbal description. Your words should marry your actions though you do not have to talk all the time or give a continuous running commentary. The more involved manoeuvres might be best completed in silence anyway. Language is important: use words that people understand.

* Encourage people to ask questions about the process (and the product) as you are demonstrating. If it is clear that you need to hold back from giving an answer for a minute whilst you complete some action they will understand.

* Adjust the speed of your movements to suit your students, especially if they are watching and copying, ie the 'do it with me' type of demonstration.

4 Once you have finished demonstrating, you will need to check the process has been understood. There are a number of ways you can do this:

* Ask students to check with one another that they do know what to do by showing each other or talking it through. One may have missed a point and feel happier about asking a colleague than showing his/her 'ignorance' in front of the group.

* Ask if there are any points that people are not sure about and if they would like you to go over anything again ... even offer to show them the whole thing again if it is feasible.

* Ask students to recap the main points — verbalising the process will help reinforce their learning.

5 Individual practice and supervision is covered in the next section. Your observation and assessment of people's attempts to carry out the activity that you have just demonstrated is the best test of whether they have understood. On the basis of what you see them do, you can assess their proficiency both as individuals and as a group and modify what you do next as follows:

* Repeat the demonstration so that everyone can review the main points.

* Invite a more competent member of the group to demonstrate whilst you comment upon what s/he is doing, as a way of reinforcing for others what you yourself have done earlier. (Take care not to embarrass any individual in this way or set up any sense of competition in the group.)

* Have an informal discussion of what the group finds easy ... or hard ... or fun ... or impossible!

6 Finish the demonstration part of your session with a word of encouragement to help people to carry on on their own. The chances are that you did not find it that easy when you first started to do it, so tell them so, including the laughable mistakes that you made. Give out any printed material or handout setting out the main points if you have not already done so.

KEY POINTS

❑ **Prepare for your demonstration by breaking it down into appropriate stages that people will understand and be able to cope with.**

❑ **Check often that people can see what you are doing and that they understand how each part fits into the whole.**

---

12   Individual practice and supervision

It is obvious to all that use and practice of a new skill, action or idea will improve performance. However, the important point for you as tutor is not only that you provide your students with opportunities to try something out which they may not be able to do elsewhere but that you can also give them individual help and encouragement. Such supervised practice may well be the optimum learning procedure.

1   Participants should know exactly what they are to do. Even where the practice follows directly on a demonstration you should specify clearly what you want individuals to do.

   * Plan specific times during a session when individual practice is to be undertaken. Warn students so that they can come properly prepared.

   * Arrange the environment with care. If it means changing rooms, moving furniture, sweeping floors, altering the ventilation, lighting, heating and so on, then do so. Ideally, such things should be done before students arrive but reality may dictate otherwise. Negotiate with the group and devise some system where all knuckle down to prepare the setting together (and undertake to put it back afterwards.)

   * Inject enthusiasm and enjoyment into the proceedings and emphasise the benefits that can and should accrue. Warn the group that they may not do it perfectly first time but that you feel sure that everyone should be able to make a fair stab at it.

   * Ensure that people are employing the correct procedure from the start, even where you have decided that you are going to 'shape' their behaviour from a basic approximation to a honed product. It may be difficult to correct learnt mistakes once an individual feels s/he is well on the way to success.

   * Organise things so that opportunities for competition are minimal for there may be some individuals who secretly *want to be best*. Talking this through with the group beforehand will help and so will positioning people carefully in the room, though one or two may still need a gentle, private word from you.

2 When supervising, observe and/or listen to each person in order to diagnose what they are doing. Make an assessment in terms of their previous performance, the nature and difficulty of the new activity, and what you judge them to be capable of. Allocate your time fairly amongst individuals. Adults will not expect equal time from you every session but they will expect you to be fair overall. Guard against giving too much attention to particular individuals at the expense of the majority.

3 Be conscious of the group as a whole, even when you are dealing with one person at a time. Listen and watch in case some or all are bored, mystified or ready for more. If you see or hear that others want your assistance, acknowledge their requests and indicate that you will get round to them. There is no reason why they should not seek advice and comment from others near them. However, watch out for the group 'expert' who may go on a 'circular tour' of his/her own, dispensing incorrect advice and unhelpful comments.

4 Encourage individuals, whilst making sure that the quality of performance they are aiming for is within their potential capacity. Find out what they think about what they are doing and praise them for trying as well as achieving. Give specific hints and guidelines rather than vague assurances. (See *Chapter 21: Assessment.*)

5 The whole purpose of an individual practising any activity is to be able do it more efficiently and effectively. When and where people begin to experience positive effects and/or achieve something they see to be worthwhile, their own achievement will spur them to further success. Until then, you will need to reward and reinforce their attempts.

6 Here are forty-nine ways of saying **good** that you might use:

> 1   *I like that!*
> 2   *That's right!*
> 3   *That's the way!*
> 4   *You're doing fine!*
> 5   *Nice going!*
> 6   *That's coming along nicely!*
> 7   *That's great!*
> 8   *Terrific!*
> 9   *Good work!*

10   *That's better!*
11   *Excellent!*
12   *Smashing!*
13   *Good going!*
14   *Keep it up!*
15   *That's really nice!*
16   *Keep up the good work!*
17   *Much better!*
18   *Good for you!*
19   *That's very much better!*
20   *Exactly right!*
21   *That's a good idea!*
22   *You are doing really well!*
23   *Superb!*
24   *I knew you could!*
25   *Keep at it — it's coming on!*
26   *You're really working hard today!*
27   *You're doing that beautifully!*
28   *That's it!*
29   *That's good!*
30   *That's the way to do it!*
31   *You are really learning a lot!*
32   *That's better than ever!*
33   *Fine!*
34   *Now that is good. Well done!*
35   *You remembered!*
36   *You're really improving!*
37   *I really think you've got it!*
38   *Well, look at you!*
39   *Tremendous!*
40   *I do like that!*
41   *Great!*
42   *You did that very well!*
43   *Congratulations!*
44   *That was first class!*
45   *Well done!*
46   *You've cracked it!*
47   *One more time and you've got it!*
48   *You must have been practising!*
49   *Wow!*

KEY POINTS

❑　Be forthcoming with your praise without be-
　　ing insincere; people need specific encourage-
　　ment and rewards.

❑　Avoid competition between students but there
　　is nothing wrong with pointing out someone
　　who is doing well or trying hard.

13   Discussion

One of the most enjoyable features of adult education is meeting other people and sharing knowledge and experience. Discussion is a planned for and managed event where a group of people jointly explore a topic, area of knowledge or a set of attitudes. It is often preceded by a specific task or activity acting as a stimulus and it requires a clear aim and a set of learning objectives. It follows that purposeful discussion rarely occurs spontaneously in a group without the tutor doing something more than suggesting it should take place.

1   There is evidence that group discussion can be effective in modifying people's attitudes, particularly where the group leader is seen to be a 'credible communicator'. Where people are presented with new ideas and beliefs that are contrary to their previous experience, it appears easier to modify their attitudes within the supportive context of a group than where they are individual members of a passive audience. Discussion within a group can enable individuals to gain confidence in themselves and in their opinions. At the same time it can also be useful in helping group members arrive at a clearer understanding of a topic, whether or not they subsequently modify their behaviours.

2   However, the method does have limitations. As tutor you will need to be aware that many adults do not find it easy to join in open group discussions and indeed they may be averse to the whole idea. They may prefer *to be taught* and you will have to provide sympathetic encouragement and support to persuade them to participate.

3   Although group discussion can promote learning and attitude change, it is not a very effective way of presenting information. Yet without a core of received knowledge, a discussion can degenerate into pooled ignorance. You will therefore need to guide and encourage students' reading and learning to the point where they can actively participate to some purpose.

4   The following points suggest how you might set about preparing for worthwhile discussions:

   *   Determine the objectives of the particular discussion. What is it that you intend that each individual should be able to do, or think or feel

as a result of taking part? Identify the topic and the purpose of the discussion some time before so that students know what they will be talking about and why.

* If the discussion is to follow on from a film, a talk, a demonstration, some reading, then decide upon the specific theme(s) you want to consider and design specific questions to structure the subsequent discussion. Alternatively, plan a task or activity which people can begin with, perhaps working in small groups of two, three or four. Whichever way you do it, you will need to provide a clear structure and a starting point; people should have an orientation period before they begin.

* Groups need to be large enough to include a variety of opinions and experience, yet small enough to allow each individual to feel that s/he can safely make a contribution. With a group as large as 20, it would help if you broke it down into two smaller groups. This will encourage the less confident and draw upon everyone's view point. Find someone suitable from each group to act as 'chair'/facilitator. You could combine the groups later in the session, ask for a summary of the ideas and opinions that emerged from each and then try to draw some general conclusions from what was said.

* Get the environment right. To facilitate the free flow of ideas, arrange the chairs in an informal way — a close U-shape or circle, without desks but with gaps to let people in and out. Get people comfortably seated; avoid having them sitting (or hiding) behind each other. Try to avoid old antagonists sitting directly opposite each other, or cliques sitting together.

* There is no optimum period of time for a discussion. It depends upon the topic, the group and how much total time you have available. When you prepare for the session, decide how much time you think you should devote to it, check that the objectives you have in mind are achievable within the time-scale, then stick to it.

5 You will need to actively manage what is going on, supporting, guiding and encouraging your students.

* Make selective use of questions to encourage quieter people to contribute. It might be useful at the start to ask what they *feel* about

something rather than what they *think*; this may seem less threatening to them. Silences do not have to be filled. Most people need time to absorb and reflect upon what has just been said by others and to think through how they react to it.

* Treat your students' viewpoints with respect — even though you may disagree with some of the information they offer or the attitudes they express. On the other hand, you should challenge statements which display obvious racist, sexist and other derogatory attitudes, if others do not do so.

* One of your main functions, once members of the group are actively participating, is to keep them focused on the topic and to ensure that their contributions are relevant and purposeful. Therefore, you should:
  − clarify vague or confusing remarks
  − query obvious misconceptions and wrong ideas if others do not
  − confirm that everyone understands what is being said
  − ask contributors to substantiate statements, especially where they show undue prejudice and rigid attitudes
  − note down the important points so that you can refer to them later.

6 Discussions can easily fade away, though on some occasions people become so enthusiastic and interested it is difficult to stop them.

* Call a halt to the proceedings at the right moment. Ideally this will be at a 'natural break' in the discussion, around the time you have decided to stop.

* Summarise what has been discussed, reviewing the main points. You might also consider making a written summary as a handout for the group. One of the students might be willing to do this if you have agreed it beforehand, though the task could prevent him/her from contributing much as s/he may well want to take notes.

* Make certain that you move things on. The discussion had a purpose and presumably you are going to make use of the outcomes later; indicate how and why.

* Thank people for having taken part and find time to speak to anyone who has made a particularly useful contribution, has participated for the first time, has seemed unusually quiet, or has obviously enjoyed it.

* Once you are on your own, evaluate what you think has been achieved. Consider which individuals may have learnt something, changed their attitudes, or become more confident as a result of the activity. Decide how you might modify the way you managed this method on another occasion.

KEY POINTS

❑ **Be clear in your own mind what you want people to achieve as a result of a 'formal' discussion before you initiate one.**

❑ **Monitor the process carefully and summarise the main outcomes at the end.**

---

14   Other methods

Panel/debate

What is it?

A number of expert guests or knowledgeable group members respond to questions or hold a dicussion in front of the group.

A debate involves the presentation of cases plus subsequent arguments and defence.

Value to students

- Different view points contrasted
- Removes tutor from centre
- Other groups can be invited
- Provides direct contact with eminent individuals and important ideas

Points to note

- Invite good speakers who are experts
- Brief panel as to group level, interest and intended objectives
- Ask the group to prepare questions for the panel
- Ensure the group has background knowledge
- Appoint a good chair.

Small group task

What is it?

Small groups carry out a specific task or activity. It can involve problem-solving, discussion, practical work or physical activity.

Value to students

- Encourages inter-personal co-operation
- People learn from each other
- Encourages participation in a small, safe environment

Points to note

- Clarify the task: ensure everyone understands
- Monitor progress
- Allow sufficient time for reporting and feedback
- Record the important points.

Brainstorming

What is it?

The tutor asks for a list of ideas, proposals, suggestions related to a particular theme. The aim is to produce a comprehensive list which can be analysed and used as the basis of a subsequent task or activity.

Value to students
- Every contribution is of equal value
- Stimulates ideas
- Involves everyone
- Uses their experience

Points to note
- Encourage people to produce ideas quickly
- Record responses accurately
- Avoid making judgments on individual contributions
- Keep to time limit.

Buzz group

What is it?

Pairs or trios discuss a particular question or short topic very briefly. It can be repeated several times in a session.

Value to students
- Can provide a prelude and/or a 'break' in a presentation
- Useful and quick way to involve people
- Focuses attention on the topic in hand
- Checks out ideas, level of understanding and progress

Points to note
- Ensure the topic is clear
- Keep people to the task in hand
- Make it fun and 'punchy': watch the time
- Ask what they've come up with but do not use any formal feedback procedures
- Get them to work with other partners if repeated.

Visit/field trip

What is it?
Students as individuals or as a group visit a venue relevant to the course. It can involve interviewing people, finding information, handling artifacts, observing a process, or putting theory or skills into practice.

Value to students
- It is reality
- Enhances motivation and interest
- Chance to gain first-hand experience to take back and discuss later

Points to note
- Organise it carefully
- Make a preliminary inspection visit
- Prepare the group; negotiate and agree the ground rules
- Allow time for debriefing and discussion of visit.

Case study

What is it?
The important details of an event or set of circumstances are presented in written or visual form for the group to diagnose, analyse or solve a problem.

Value to students
- Brings real life situations into the classroom
- Can test existing knowledge and learning accurately
- Enhances interest and participation
- Improves ability to identify underlying principles and processes

Points to note
- Make the case relevant, topical and straightforward
- Research the material
- Have clear learning outcomes
- Follow it with a discussion or other activity relating it to real practice.

Role play

What is it?

A short 'spontaneous' acting-out of situations where students assume specific roles. It is useful for looking at behaviour and relationships.

Value to students
- Provides insight into attitudes and feelings of others
- Encourages participation and can be fun
- Promotes importance of feelings as well as thinking and knowing

Points to note
- Let individuals opt out if they so wish
- Ensure 'drama' doesn't take over
- Leave plenty of time for debriefing and discussion
- Use the experience to move their practice on.

Simulation

What is it?

A prepared and structured 'simulation' of a real situation. Roles, materials and background details are provided for each participant. It may be modified as it proceeds by the addition of further information.

Value to students
- Produces considerable involvement and commitment to the 'characters'
- Leads to insight into other people's actions
- Has the potential to initiate reappraisal of other people's perceptions

Points to note
- Allow time for considerable preparation, perhaps with outline scripts
- Make it realistic; use props
- Agree the ground rules and insist they are adhered to; supervise precisely
- Leave plenty of time for debriefing and discussion.

Games

What is it?
Large and small groups play an 'educational game' reminiscent of Monopoly or card games with some degree of chance. It may be commercial or 'home-grown' and can focus on problem-solving, decision-making or team work.

Value to students
- Can be very enjoyable
- People learn through doing
- Can encourage inductive and deductive thought
- Helps draw links between 'theory' and 'practice'

Points to note
- Have clear objectives
- Pilot it carefully first; ensure you know the rules yourself!
- Supervise carefully in case it gets too boisterous
- Draw out the implications and principles at the end.

Seminar

What is it?
This is an opportunity to provide new information or further clarification. It is usually led by a student who has prepared a paper (or demonstration) to give to the rest. It is usually followed by question and answer, and/or a discussion.

Value to students
- Stimulates an individual to research a topic in depth
- Shares responsibility for 'teaching' with the whole group
- Can result in worthwhile and critical discussion
- Gives individuals experience of leading/teaching a group

Points to note
- Specify/negotiate the topics well in advance
- Advise and support the students prior to and during the session
- Request the group to do some preparatory work
- Watch for a tendency of the rest to switch off when it's not their turn.

Tutorial

What is it?

This is an arranged, planned-for discussion between a student (or 2/3 maximum) and tutor. It is usually supervisory in some way with an individually agreed purpose, agenda and time scale.

Value to students
- Allows student to follow up his/her particular needs, ideas and feelings
- Provides personal support and confirmation
- Provides the individual with a 'yard-stick' for his/her progress

Points to note
- Make it a dialogue between equal adults
- Provide private, comfortable and secure environment
- Be prepared and aware of student's likely needs
- Negotiate and agree any action plans.

Individual project

What is it?

A specific task(s) is undertaken by an individual or small group. This may be the major reason why a student attends the course especially in practical subjects.

Value to students
- Initiative is with the students(s)
- Likely to be highly motivating
- Produces tangible outcome
- Promotes co-operation with others when in a group situation

Points to note
- Ensure it is relevant to and attainable by the student
- Check 'on-going' progress regularly and give constructive feedback
- Be aware that individual projects can make students resent time spent on what seem to be 'irrelevant' teaching episodes.

Diary

What is it?

Students keep a personal record of their progress, their practice regime, their responses to course sessions, other themes or problems.

Value to students
- Helps develop self-awareness and self-assessment
- Relates the course to other parts of the students' lives
- Provides evidence on aspects of personal behaviour which can be analysed and discussed

Points to note
- Check that diaries do not become just descriptive without any analysis
- Set ground rules right at the start; avoid breaching any contract of privacy
- Negotiate with students how to monitor whether they are continuing to make entries.

Work between sessions

What is it?

Individuals work or study between group meetings. This can take the form of reading, writing or some other activity, such as collecting newspaper items, making a taped 'radio-type' programme or interview, critically watching a TV programme, collecting artifacts, listening to a tape, etc.

Value to students
- Keeps continuity and interest between sessions
- Allows students to work at their own pace in their own time
- Encourages those who want to stretch themselves

Points to note
- Encourage people to do some sort of homework
- Specify the task(s) clearly, saying if, how and when it is to be assessed
- Offer help with ideas and resources
- Provide an early opportunity to discuss and share any work done.

KEY POINTS

❑ Consciously select methods which will best help your students to learn the particular content or skill.

❑ Give time and thought to the preparation and management of the method you have chosen so that you will know how, when and where to use it in the session.

15   Working with groups

A great deal has been written about the social psychology of groups, the way they form, the roles individuals play and how people interact. However, a teaching group is a special kind of group in so far as there is a *de facto* leader from the start — the tutor. Consequently, the usual social/psychological processes are subordinate to the particular learning tasks of individual members, whether or not they are working co-operatively. As to the size of a learning/teaching group, most sessional classes in adult, community or further education are between 12-20, though a few may be slightly larger where demand is high. We have therefore taken a 'large group' to refer to this range, and 'small group(s)' to mean a sub-division of three to six people.

Many of the methods employed by adult education tutors are designed to work with small numbers of people though they will work equally well with a large group. Whatever the actual size of a group of adult students, the tutor's first task is to create a climate where interaction can flourish, where people can participate in safety and learn both with and from others. What follows here are some general thoughts about groups plus some suggestions about managing small group work.

1   The difference between a class of adult students and a group made up of the same individuals is that members of the latter will actively relate and learn from each other as well as from the tutor. Being part of a group satisfies people's need for a sense of security and belonging, for giving and receiving attention, for being favourably regarded and for being stimulated by and learning from others. Groups can provide a supportive atmosphere for individual practice, experimentation and innovation. They help people reconsider and modify their attitudes and approaches, as well as producing more varied and more stimulating ideas than can individuals working alone.

2   You should facilitate the group so that these processes happen and then capitalise upon them. As individuals come to trust others in the group, they should be more willing to participate in a wider range of learning tasks and activities. As tutor, you have the responsibility for organising and managing these activities in ways that will extend and develop individual group members.

3 However, there are a number of potential difficulties which you may have to resolve:

   – coping with the dominant (and quiet) group member
   – the potential embarrassment of personal self-disclosure
   – the subsequent reluctance of members to work on their own
   – over-concern for the emotional/social life of the group by some group members
   – the development of sub-groups and cliques
   – the emergence of unacceptable group norms
   – integrating new students
   – coping with those who do not want to join in.

These are issues both for you and the group, and in an ideal world they should be resolved jointly. However, the reality is that where something becomes problematic, students usually expect the tutor to resolve the crisis.

4 There are a number of ways in which you can begin the process of group formation with your adult students. Some of the more important points — about using names, introducing people to one another and the use of 'icebreakers' — are covered in Chapter 23 (*The first session*). However, they all have to do with people getting to know each other and feeling less isolated. The crucial feature is that you should make it easy for people to use their normal social skills in what may seem a potentially threatening setting — a classroom with a teacher present!

When you decide to use a teaching method which involves your students working in small groups, chosen either from the methods described in this book or from elsewhere, there are a number of general pointers that you might find worth considering. The fact that the group is used to working in such ways does not obviate the need for preparing thoroughly and acting upon identified management and process issues.

5 You will need to decide what small group size is best. In part this will depend upon what you want your students to do, but it will also depend upon how much time you have, how big the group is and whether you have odd or even numbers. (You will not be certain until you can count them in front of you!). There are no hard and fast rules except that as group size increases from two to six, so the time required to do the task also increases though this is balanced by having fewer groups to report

back. If you choose pairs or trios or quartets, decide what you are going to do with a student who is 'left out'.

* You must decide the composition of each group — is it to be a free-for-all, or *work with someone you know well*, or *someone you haven't yet worked with*? Do you want to arrange the groups according to people's backgrounds, personalities and/or experience or should students decide how they are to group themselves? Again, there are no definitive rules; you must decide on the basis of the particular outcomes you want, aware that you may well make a quite different choice for the next small group activity.

6 Where equipment is involved in small group work ensure there will be enough to go round whether it is pens or video cameras. People will get involved in the activity and will not want to be bothered by requests from other groups.

* Make sure all equipment is working and that you know how to handle it correctly (and can carry out running repairs). Even though you have checked it before the session starts, have a spare ready just in case.

* Give people time to familiarise themselves with any novel piece of equipment, especially if it appears complicated. Make use of the students who know to help those who do not, but watch out for those who impose their superior knowledge on the less experienced.

7 Telling people just once what you want them to do and how you want them to do it is rarely sufficient! Some might not hear the task correctly; others will forget what you said. Try telling them what the task is first and once that is clear tell them 'how'. Better still, write the task down on a handout or flip-chart as well. Ask if there are any questions or queries, and even where there are none, you might still outline the main features again. As people are organising themselves, be on hand to advise, move the odd chair and gently facilitate getting everyone started.

8 Decide how you are going to monitor what is taking place in each small group. You can walk round quietly every so often, listening unobtrusively or you can actually sit in with each group for a while. (If you do join a group, be aware that you will alter the dynamic and they may defer to you.) If you are happy with what people are doing let them get

on with it. If you discover that there is a general misunderstanding then make a brief general announcement; if it's just one group, quietly tell them, though the choice to continue discussing what they are discussing is actually theirs. Though no one may need you as they are all happy getting on, do not leave the room, as your absence will be adversely noted. Use the time quietly to get ready for the next part of the session. Warn everyone when they have 'x' minutes remaining.

9   You must value the work that each group has done even though the real benefit may be the group work itself rather than the feedback to the whole group. Avoid asking every group to share everything — it becomes tedious, but where you must, choose the group that you judge will be brief and to the point to go first. They will be the model for the rest. Better still:

 - request each group to select/prioritise two or three of the more important points they have agreed. Then ask each in turn for one point, moving on to the next group for theirs and so on. This way everyone will be able to make a contribution, choosing a second or a third item if their 'first' has already been offered by another group.
 - choose one group at random or let them draw playing cards from a pack (or numbers from a hat, or spills from a book) asking just them to describe what they did. Other groups then add on any additional items or ideas that they have come up with
 - give each group one sheet of flipchart paper (or an OHP acetate) and ask them to itemise their findings. Show them a 'mock-up' so they can see that you only want 'x' lines, written *this big* set out *like this*
 - collect in a written *précis* (in clear, black handwriting) from each group and photocopy them for the rest.

 *   With individual and pair work you are unlikely to want everyone to feedback everything, so ask for one thing from each person or pair and/or give each a strip of card or paper to write down their 'best' point and ask them to display it using a drawing pin, Blu-tack or velcro board.

 *   The major problem is making sense of the ideas as they flow in and using them thereafter. One way is to think through beforehand the range of responses you are likely to get and prepare one or more areas on the board or flip chart in which to write them. This way, you can categorise the groups' ideas as they present them, making it much easier for you to use them in the next step. If during the process of

writing up you shorten or edit what people say, check that they are happy with the new wording.

* You might try 'snowballing' as something different. Ask each individual to identify four of her/his points; then negotiate with a partner over the combined 8 (2x4) to end up with three for the pair of them. Two pairs then negotiate their combined 6 (2x3) to produce two for the quartet ... two quartets then combine their 4 (2x2) to give one. You will have to work out the numbers of points to be negotiated at each stage, depending upon how many people you have to start with. You can, if you wish, end up with two, three or four points, to be voted on by the group as a whole. Make this activity fun and do not let people agonise over their choices: keep it moving like a game of musical chairs.

10 Methods that are likely to involve personal identification and/or emotional responses (role play, simulation and other so-called 'experiential' methods), will require particularly careful management.

* Tell the group the topic area that is to be focused upon and exactly what they are to be asked to do. You must give them the freedom to opt out if they wish, in ways that do not cause embarrassment. If it is appropriate give them a demonstration. (If you need a 'stooge', agree it with that individual beforehand.) Let people remain sitting comfortably while you explain things rather than have them standing around feeling sheepish. Make it clear when they are to start ... and how and when you will stop them.

* Provide a 'debriefing' time as soon as the active part is over. Give people the chance to unwind by telling their partner(s) or you, or the group, how they felt about the experience, especially if it has engendered any antagonistic feeling towards other 'actors'. Do not rush this period; it is important to individuals and you may be able to use some of the points later in the session.

11 The major weakness of these particular types of 'experiential' methods is that many tutors fail to capitalise on the outcomes. Once people have experienced 'what it feels like', or recognised 'what can happen', you must help them to take this awareness further through some additional discussion and/or activity. Knowing 'what it is like' does not automatically equip people to act more appropriately.

KEY POINTS

❑　Facilitate relationships and procedures within the group at the start.

❑　Actively manage small group work with tact and sensitivity, first having made it clear exactly what you want students to do.

16   Asking questions

Though asking questions may not normally be categorised as a teaching method in the way that lecturing and role play are, it plays a significant part in helping people learn. All tutors are likely to ask questions in their teaching regardless of the particular method they are using. As questions play such an important part in helping students think and learn, consider the following:

1   Questions are intended to evoke responses from individuals — mentally and usually verbally. When you ask a question you should be clear in your own mind what purpose or purposes you intend it to serve. They can include:

   – stimulating interest, motivation and curiosity
   – eliciting student knowledge for the benefit of others
   – checking and assessing levels of understanding
   – focusing thinking
   – developing/stimulating logical and critical thought
   – developing self-expression of thought and of feeling
   – involving individuals and adding variety
   – encouraging communication between group members.

2   One way of classifying questions involves the type of thinking processes required to answer them. These are *recall, observation* and *thought*, though in truth they can often merge into one another. Some questions can also be described as *closed* where they usually require brief, specific answers; others are known as *open* and require more extended answers.

3   The process of asking questions involves various tactics, regardless of whether the tutor is trying to assess knowledge, develop thought or whatever. Here are some suggestions you may find helpful when you ask questions:

   *   Make the question clear and brief, asking one thing at a time. Avoid questions which require a long introduction or an explanation to make them comprehensible. Sequence questions if you intend to ask more than one. Begin with the easier ones before asking those which require more thought. Avoid random and arbitrary questions or those which require mind reading on the part of students.

* Choose the right focus and pitch. Open questions usually require broad and extended answers and they are likely to promote further discussion. Closed questions call for narrowly focused answers and they are useful for drawing out specific facts, promoting deductive and logical thought. Pitch your questions at the right level for the individual and the group, using words and concepts they understand.

* Questions should be directed to the group as a whole, though you may wish to ask questions of specific individuals on occasion. Make it clear to people what you intend and do not address your questions to the ceiling or your finger nails. Phrase questions so that everyone has a chance to grasp them and ask those who look ready to answer. Try to avoid asking those who always know and take care how you handle people who are normally rather quiet.

* Be encouraging and sympathetic in the way you actually ask a question. Too threatening or direct a manner will raise people's level of anxiety.

* Pause to give people time to answer. They will need space to think about the question and to work out what they are going to say. Learn to cope with thinking silences.

* Respond to people's answers with warmth and enthusiasm. If you are encouraging in the way you react, they will be more likely to contribute again. Use non-verbal as well as verbal signals — look at them, smile and nod.

* Support individuals who are struggling to answer a question. Give them more time by rephrasing the question or gently suggesting a likely area of response. Where the answer is incorrect take care not to put the person down, though you should not collude with a wrong response: indicate the type of answer you are after. Alternatively, ask a different (simpler/more direct) question of the individual or perhaps ask others if they would like to add anything or modify the answer. Find an opportunity later to value the person who gave a wrong answer for a subsequent correct response or for some other piece of positive behaviour.

* Where you find it difficult to understand a response to your question, be honest and ask the individual to repeat and/or rephrase and/or explain it further. This will be to the benefit of the rest of the group since it is likely they will not have understood it either.

* Refer back to individual answers made earlier in the session — *as Mary said .... and as Parveen told us* . This will help knit the group together, value student contributions and boost individual egos. Where it is appropriate, use the responses from individuals to construct a framework of ideas and understanding. You could make a note of important responses on the board; this will encourage participation and ownership of the material under consideration.

4 Questioning involves people and encourages them to participate, but to use it solely for this purpose is to undervalue its full potential. Make frequent and thoughtful use of questions to help your students focus their thinking and develop their understanding of what they are learning with you.

KEY POINTS

❏ **Be patient; what is a simple question to you may require considerable thought for some students.**

❏ **Avoid asking trivial and unanswerable questions; ask only those that will carry the teaching and learning process forward.**

---

17 Teaching resources

Using teaching resources, whether they be audio visual aids, materials, people, objects or events, not only makes the whole classroom process more interesting and enjoyable but they actually do help teachers to teach more effectively and adults students to learn more efficiently. This is not to say that every session requires a pantechnicon of aids and resources; in some cases they might actively detract from what is being addressed. The choices of what to use and when depend upon a number of factors, including:

- the particular properties of a resource that will enhance learning
- the 'cost-benefit' outcome: increased student learning versus the tutor time, cost and effort put into its manufacture
- the likely response from the group to a particular resource
- the level of tutor experience and skill in using the item.

There are several texts available on the use of teaching resources in general and audio-visual aids (AVA) in particular. Several manufacturers of equipment, notably of overhead projectors, produce useful pamphlets containing hints and ideas. What follows here are several general points about the use of teaching resources and a comprehensive list of 'items'. A random inventory of some novel uses of teaching resources is also included together with a 'teaching box' check list.

1   The quality of all teaching resources is important. Take time and trouble to produce or acquire items of good quality that are big enough and clear enough for people to see and hear. If it is apparent to your students that you have not bothered very much then their motivation and interest will be affected. When you manufacture something worthwhile, store it away carefully to use another time.

2   Make sure you know how to use the resource. Work on the principle that if AVA technology can go wrong, it will. Find out how to operate that particular model or item in advance and discover how to replace bulbs, fuses, etc. Check that it is working before any students arrive and identify the best working position in the room and the optimum seating plan for its use.

3　Have an alternative strategy available if for some reason key AVA or resources are not available — a bulb and its replacement both blow; material is not photocopied in time; a visitor fails to turn up.

4　Enlist the the help of the students in your class. Each will have a houseful of objects, a wealth of ideas and experience and a desire to suggest alternative resources. Few will be unwilling to 'bring and show' some object or lend it to you. Some will have particular skills and may well be willing to construct something for your use with the group.

5　The odd and unusual item will gain attention and help people learn. Look out for the variety of objects and visual ideas that others use in their classrooms and take note of what you see on television, at work, around the home and in the toy and hobby shop. Steal ideas unashamedly and adapt them to your purpose. Be creative in the ways you use AVA and resources — think 'laterally'.

6　Some learning resources:

People

Yourself	Other tutors	Centre head/principal
Your students	Centre/college staff	Friends and relations
Manufacturers	Shop owners/managers	Other 'professionals'

Resource Materials

Books	Catalogues	Advertisements
Tutor manuals	Photocopies	Promotional literature
Reports	Information notes	Publicity material
Handouts	Periodicals/journals	Newspapers
Magazines	Comics	Original documents

Audio/Visual Aids

Writing boards	Magnetic boards	Video recorder
Charts/posters	Tape recorder	Slide projector
Photographs	Record player	Film projector
Flip chart	Radio	Overhead projector
Display board	Television	Epidiascope
Flannel/velcro boards	Video camera	Microscope

Objects

The 'real thing'	Models	Samples
Specimens	Toys	A volunteer

Outside events and visits

Museums	Lectures	Sports/leisure centres
Exhibitions	Field trips	Cinema/theatre/concert
Conferences	Specialist shops	

(See *Chapter 25: Working with large groups* for some additional guide-lines about audio-visual hardware, projections, and students note-taking.)

7 Here are some are some unusual teaching resource ideas that have been used with adult groups. If you can employ any of them, well and good, but it is more important that you use them as a catalyst for developing your own ideas:

 – Have a collection of old hats for role play.

 – Keep all your handout and OHP master sheets in plastic envelopes in a ring binder.

 – Store OHP acetates in a ring binder, interleaved with paper and catalogued with labelled section dividers.

 – Have a teddy bear to represent an emotive figure — a deceased relative, an accident victim or an aggressive colleague.

 – Put up a large blown-up photograph of the individual writer being discussed.

 – Play mood music before the session: *Pictures at an Exhibition* in a painting class?

 – Hang up an adapted nursery mobile to represent a process in equilibrium.

 – Give out steel baking trays with stylised strip-magnetised pieces to find the positions of a sailing yacht with regard to wind, tide and estuary buoys.

 – Keep a handful of 6"x4" blank record cards for a spontaneous group activity: it will look more prepared-for than asking students to find a bit of paper.

 – Build up a book box 'library'. Start with a few well-labelled books of your own and ask students to pay a small fee when they borrow something and use the cash to buy additional 'book box books' — label new ones appropriately!

- Cut out line drawings and cartoons from local newspaper adverts and articles and use them to illustrate your photocopied handouts and OHP transparencies.

- Write to major manufacturers for (free) samples not only of their finished products and/or publicity materials but also for samples of the raw materials they use.

- Burn a marked candle in a water saucer to represent a time span.

- Use 'Post-it' memos to collect and display ideas from the group ... and use them as the adhesive power to put up bigger sheets of paper as 'disclosure covers' on a prepared poster or as add-on items for a chart.

- Place coins on an OHP as movable elements in silhouette.

- Photocopy 35mm slides for your own reference and as handouts.

- Cut out balsa wood shapes and letters to make a three-dimensional chart.

- Paste sticky paper on cheap playing cards and use them to distribute roles/activities/tasks/ running order etc ... students to choose one from the 'fan' you hold out.

- Take 35mm slides of all and any aspect of your subject for later use in class.

- Design a personal logo to identify all your handouts — have a rubber stamp made.

- Tip a largish table up-end and rest an edge on a chair for use as a flip chart stand.

- Use Polyfilla to make simple models: paint them with emulsion and water colours.

- Use a photocopier several times in succession to really enlarge items.

- Buy some simple sweets (Polos, wine gums) and hand them round occasionally.

- Invite a supplier/manufacturer to talk about the business from his/her perspective.

8 Never go anywhere without your teaching box! Find a suitable container — from a large pencil case to a Gladstone bag or tool 'carry-all' — for your equipment. Your subject will determine the specialist items you will need, but some of the more general items that many teachers keep by them are:

Biros	Record cards (6"x4")	Sellotape
Chalk	Receipt book	Stapler
Felt tip pens	Blank sound tapes	Staples
Highlight pens	Blank video tapes	Staple remover
OHP pens (permanent)	Screwdriver	String
OHP pen eraser	Double adaptor	Bottle/can opener
OHP pens (water based)	Extension lead	Calculator
Pencils	Fuses	Craft knife
Pencil sharpener	Spare OHP/35mm bulbs	Elastoplast
Rubber	Blu-Tack	Nail file
Tippex/Snowpake	Drawing pins	Pain-killing tablets
Whiteboard pens	Dressmaking pins	Pen knife
Card (A4)	Dog clips	Rulers
Flip chart paper	Glue stick (Pritt Stick)	Scissors
Name badges	Masking tape	Telephone card
Notepad	Needle and cotton	Torch
OHP acetates	Paper clips	Travelling clock
Paper (A4)	Safety pins	Tissues

KEY POINTS

❑ Use imaginative teaching resources and AVA to enhance people's learning and achievement.

❑ Give some time and effort to producing good AVA: they will pay dividends in student interest, motivation, learning and enjoyment.

IV   Reviewing learning

Introduction

In recent years there has been a growing interest in the process of evaluation, both within education generally and in adult education in particular. In both contexts, evaluation means describing something in appropriate terms and then judging how acceptable or suitable that something is. The 'something' may be any aspect of education, but in adult education, it is typically (a) a total programme as offered by a college, an adult education institute or a Community Service, or (b) a course or single session. In the United Kingdom, the term 'assessment' is usually reserved for describing an individual (when the 'something' can be a student or a teacher), though the terms are sometimes used interchangeably. Whichever words are used, the concept has to do with looking at a teaching/learning event with the intention of answering such questions as: *Is what is being done what is supposed to be done? Is it being done efficiently and effectively? Are the participants achieving something of value?*

Evaluation can best be seen as a way of working, part of a continuous process of observing, asking questions and offering explanations, on the basis of which changes can be made and/or existing practice confirmed. The term 'monitoring' can be used to describe the collecting of information, whilst 'evaluation' refers more specifically to the diagnostic activity — the understanding of the information which is followed in turn by appropriate action. Evaluation should be taking place all the time, and not just at the end of a session or course. The tutor needs to be taking in information throughout, making sense of what is happening and deciding what to do next.

In terms of a course (or a session) for adults, the process of evaluation will determine the extent to which:

- the learning aims and objectives are being achieved
- the students' needs and wants are being met
- the event is/was 'value for money' and 'value for time spent'
- the planning, preparation, organisation and management are/were satisfactory
- the tutor exemplifies good adult education practice.

In terms of individual students, the process of assessment will determine the extent to which a learner has achieved subject-based and/or skill-based outcomes, and that range of more 'person-based' accomplishments and satisfactions to do with striving and succeeding.

It follows that data are needed both about the quality of a course itself and about the achievement of course participants. Evidence about the course can be gleaned from a number of sources: the judgment of an external observer, the views of course participants and the self-evaluation carried out by the tutor. Evidence concerning student learning outcomes can be obtained by a variety of both formal and informal methods. Properly interpreted and acted upon, these several sources of evidence will help the tutor provide the quality of adult education that people have a right to expect.

18   Course and session evaluation

1   One way to obtain an evaluation of what is taking place on your course is for you to invite an outsider to act as an observer/evaluator of one of your sessions. Together, agree a procedure for such a visit and decide upon a set of criteria . You might also identify any aspects you would particularly like feedback about. Once the visit has taken place your 'evaluator' discusses his/her observations with you. Considerable benefit can be derived from this procedure, especially where your visitor is a colleague and you can attend each other's sessions. Not only can you give each other useful feedback but you can also pick up new ideas for use on your own course.

2   If you decide to try this out, consider the following points:

*   The colleague you team up with can be either more or less experienced than you. What s/he is able to observe and comment upon may be slightly different depending on his/her level of expertise, but the perspective offered will be equally valuable.

*   It is not vital that s/he teaches the same subject as you, unless you especially want comment about how you teach particular content. Good adult teaching transcends the subject taught and a view from someone working in another area may throw fresh light on what you do.

*   Explain to your students what you are proposing and secure their agreement. If they do not like the idea, you must respect their views.

*   Decide on the role the visitor will play during the visit — a member of the group or a quiet observer — and where s/he might best sit.

*   Rather than discuss the session immediately afterwards, meet a day or so later when you both have had time to reflect on what took place. Make some notes yourself about the session and compare your assessment with that of your visitor.

*   Try to avoid feeling defensive or threatened by what s/he has to say. When you are the visitor, make sure you listen to what the teacher says and confirm good practice as well as offer constructive criticism.

* Give the group some feedback about what the visitor had to say and what you discussed together. Pass on any compliments. Use the opportunity to find out a little more about what the group thinks about the course by asking them if they agree with the points the two of you talked about.

3   There are a variety of methods you can employ to evaluate your course using 'internal observers' — your own course participants. The problem is to find out what they really think about the course, about themselves as a student group and about you the tutor. Adult students are reluctant to voice criticisms. It may be that they remember feeling rather vulnerable in front of all-powerful teachers at school, or that they feel unsure of their capabilities as learners, or simply that they don't want to embarrass you the tutor, someone they know and like as a person. There appears to be an hierarchy of responses:

– what they will tell you in front of other members of the group
– what they will tell you privately
– what they will say within the group during your temporary absence
– what they will say to a friend at coffee time or on the way home
– what they will say to a partner or a member of their family
– what they will not tell anyone.

The skill is to get below the first two layers! You can be reasonably sure that if you ask them too directly what they think about the course, all you are likely to get are platitudes, and not many of those either. You will need to be more subtle!

4   Watch everything that happens before, during and after the session. The cues and clues of people's responses to what you do and what you ask of them are there for you to observe. Whilst body language is not everything, it can provide you with some good indicators. Similarly, the way people say things as well as what they say, the alacrity with which they attempt something, leave the room at the end of the session, and so on, can tell you quite a lot.

5   Get into the habit of listening and talking to individuals right from the start of the course. If you arrive sufficiently early and prepare everything in good time, you are free to socialise with people as they come in; you can listen to what they say to each other, too. In addition to such 'earwigging', there is no reason why you should not initiate some evaluative responses. For example, you could comment favourably on

something a person did and in the course of your conversation ask the student what s/he thought about it ... and about the session generally ... and about a particular piece of teaching or group work you attempted. Alternatively you might say that you did not especially like something you had done in the session and enquire what s/he thought about it.

6   You will, however, need to be carrying out more structured procedures to find out what the group as a whole thinks about the ongoing course. Too much formal evaluation is relegated to the last session when whatever students say will have limited value for them personally. Thus you must ask your students at strategic points during a course whether there are things they would like modified, and, if so, how? One way you could do this is by dividing them into small groups and asking each to identify one example of the things they like doing, one they feel is of particular benefit to them and one that they are less keen about. If you also ask them to identify ways in which the course might be modified to suit them, you will get suggestions that they will not feel are criticisms of you. It is important not to expose individuals and ask them to make criticisms too publicly. By encouraging them to work with one or two partners they will not only feel less vulnerable, but they will also be able to test out and validate their personal feelings and responses against those of others.

7   Give them the opportunity to complete some form of report or questionnaire both during the course and at the end. One idea is to let people talk the questions through in small groups first and then write their responses later. If you give them the option of anonymity some may be more candid — those who want to own their opinions can sign their names.

   *   You might well choose to ask general questions to get a flavour of what your students think about the course. Some useful items you could include on a questionnaire are:

   —   *One of the most useful (valuable) aspects of the course for me is/ was ... because ...*
   —   *One of the less useful (valuable) aspects of the course for me is/ was ... because ...*
   —   *The thing I like(d) best about coming on the course is/was ... because ...*
   —   *If I could change the course, I would ...because ...*
   —   *I should also like to say that ...*

If, however, you want specific answers about particular issues, you must ask specific questions. It is no good hoping that they will tell you.

* Alternatively you could ask people to make any comments they might wish:

Please make some notes of anything you would like to say about the course (so far). You might want to say something about what we have done or whether you enjoy the course, ways you think it could be improved and how people in the group could contribute to making it more successful. Please write down anything that you think I should know, especially if it will help me adapt this course/ plan the next course.

Or more simply still: *Please say anything you like about the course (so far).*

* You may find it difficult to categorise all the responses that students make to these more open questions. Burning issues will be obvious but where only a couple of people mention a particular item, it should still be worth thinking their point through to see what they are driving at and why.

* Some tutors prefer to use rating scales of one sort or another, including box ticking and multiple choice items, though such techniques may not tell you very much. (What, for example, would an average of *7/10* tell you about your communication skills?) Other types ask students to draw their responses — sketch a smile or a grimace on a face or draw a picture to represent the course. Such methods are certainly of value for students with limited literacy skills or as a general, rather more 'fun' method.

* Whatever type of question you decide to use, lay them out on the sheet with sufficient space for the answers. Take time and trouble to make it look good, indicating by its quality that you judge the procedure — and adult student views — to be important.

8 You may choose to use open plenary techniques, either in addition to, or instead of paper and pencil methods. You can ask the whole group more directly to tell you what they think about the course. There are a variety of methods you might use — buzz groups; brainstorming;

sheets of large paper round the room with a request that people write their comments under headings; small groups reporting back to the large group; everyone saying *one good thing and one less good thing* in the large group; completely free and open discussion in the large group; and so on. However, some participants at least will find these approaches very threatening and they are unlikely to be particularly forthright in what they say.

9   If you decide that you are going to use these more 'up-front' methods then you must take time to think through the management issues involved, not least of which are:

   - when it should take place in a session and what effect might it have on what else you have planned
   - how you are going to manage the activity and if you are the the most appropriate person to chair it
   - how the observations are going to be recorded
   - how the less articulate are going to be helped to make a contribution
   - what you are physically going to do while it is taking place
   - if you are going to respond to what they say, and if so, how.

10 Any end-of-course evaluation needs to take place at an appropriate time and experience would suggest that a good place to do it is during the penultimate session. If you are using questionnaires, the group can carry out any preliminary small group discussion, fill in their individual responses at home and bring them back on the final session. Group techniques will almost certainly be better sited during a next-to-last session regardless of what is said. By carrying out evaluation at such a point, the final session of the course can be planned to remedy at least one or two omissions, give you a chance to say what you think and to finish on an upbeat note.

11 Whichever particular format or combination of formats you use, and whenever you choose to use them, you must endeavour to remain objective. When people are critical it is difficult for many teachers not to take it personally. If you are using a group technique, listen quietly to what they have to say, and if you find it appropriate to explain a particular action or event, try to do so without becoming defensive. If you are reading people's questionnaires, stay calm: you have, after all, asked for their opinions and they are giving them out of respect for you. Do not deprecate their approval and praise either; it will have been meant sincerely.

12 Once you know what they have to say, you should evaluate their evaluations. Diagnose: ask yourself questions about what they have said and test out some possible explanations. Do their comments seem reasonable; do they make sense; what is the balance of opinion in the group; does the original reason you chose to do something still seem justified? Now decide what you are going to do as a result; what changes are you going to make and what practices do you feel confirmed in and want to use again?

13 At some stage you should offer the group your evaluation of the course. Tell them what you think about what has been achieved and where you think there may have been a shortfall. Say something about them as a group and about your teaching, perhaps giving some indication of what you might do differently another time. Make sure you thank them for having taken part in the evaluation process.

14 The feedback provided by a range of ongoing, formative evaluations, coupled with knowledge of the extent to which students are achieving specified learning objectives will allow you to make modifications to a course as it proceeds. You can use the feedback provided by end-of-course summative evaluations together with that concerning students' final learning outcomes to plan and improve subsequent courses. The types of evaluation procedures that you use are less important than the fact that you actually do try to find out in a variety of ways what people think about the course.

KEY POINTS

❑ **Begin the process of course evaluation from the first session.**

❑ **Use a variety of methods and procedures to identify what is happening; then act on what they tell you.**

---

19   Attendance and drop-out

A group's attendance record is sometimes held to be a clear indicator of what is taking place: how the tutor is working and what the group is or is not achieving. Whilst it cannot be denied that the pattern of attendance over time may indicate something, it is not at all clear what that something is. A number of carefully conducted researches make it plain that the reasons people attend sporadically or drop out of a course are quite varied and that many of them have little to do with the nature or the quality of the educational experience they are being offered. That is not to say that there is no relationship between the two, for both common sense (and research) would suggest that there is. Should there be a marked decrease in regular attendance during one of your courses, it may indicate that there is some aspect(s) which you might beneficially review.

1   Taken as a whole, the data suggests that at least half of the reasons why people drop out of adult education (and about 20% do) has to do with 'personal reasons'. The range of points ex-students make is enormous, though a proportion have to do with their perceptions of their poor self-confidence as learners and their inability to integrate comfortably into a learning group.

   * Up to a quarter of the reasons given reflect a feeling that the course is not what people expected. To some extent the tutor does have some responsibility here. You should ensure that your courses are described as accurately as possible and you should try to make it clear to people at enrolment or within the first session what the course you have planned is about and at what level you hope to work. Your best efforts notwithstanding, people may still attend under misapprehensions about their capabilities and stamina to stay with the course.

   * However, up to a quarter of the reasons people give do directly relate to the tutor; adult students are frighteningly perceptive and articulate about those aspects of teacher behaviour that they find unacceptable. Their criticisms range from our inability to cope with the content matter, pitch it at an appropriate level and use comprehensible language, to our poor communication skills, lack of enthusiasm and an unwillingness to relate to people.

2   It is easy to become 'paranoid' about variations in attendance figures, especially if you teach a course regularly over a long period . It is easy to concoct all sorts of reasons why one or another person has not come and it is always possible to imagine that there was something in the previous session that you did badly, or that upset them, or that got in the way of their achievement. You may be right, but it is unlikely to have been that terrible. Students do have existences beyond adult education and the rest of their lives sometimes take priority over *your* course! However, you might think about the following strategies:

*   Agree with your students that where they can, they will try to let you know if they are going to miss a session so that you can save a handout for them ... or reserve time for them when they do next come ... or modify the session so that they will not totally miss out on a critical piece of learning.

*   Follow up any unexplained or lengthy absence with a postcard ... or a message via a friend ... or even a brief telephone call.

*   Ensure you find time for them when they next appear. Ask how they have been and brief them about what they have missed. Negotiate with them about how you can best help them catch up.

3   The fact remains, however, that a significant drop-out rate might be saying something about the course or about you. If this is the case, then the chances are that the rest of the group will know why. Share your misgivings and concern with those who remain without embarrassing them, and try to identify not only what the problem(s) may be but how it might be remedied. You may feel able to write to those who have dropped out and ask them more directly, but that might be rather difficult to do. You certainly could drop them a line and say that you have had discussion with the rest of the group, modified the course as a result, and would be delighted to see them back if they would like to come next time.

4   Because you regularly have full attendance does not mean that you should assume your course is problem-free. They may be coming because there is no alternative provision in your subject locally, or the equipment is quite good or you happen to run a highly competitive resources supply service. One student was heard to say as she left: *He doesn't get any better, but at least it's warm and the tools are sharp ... and I suppose I do learn something from watching what the rest do so the time isn't totally wasted!*

KEY POINTS

❑ Follow up absences sensitively, making it plain to people that you are looking forward to seeing them next time.

❑ Give thought to any unexplained drop-outs and what they might be saying about you, the group and/or the course.

20   Self-evaluation

An additional and very valuable way of evaluating a course is for the tutor to do it him/herself. This will not only help to evaluate the course structure, content and student achievement, but it will also help a tutor to reflect upon his/her teaching and management skills.

Such self-evaluation or self-assessment (the terms in this instance *are* interchangeable) can be carried out at a number of levels. You can make judgments about how you are working with individual students, how you taught a particular session, and about your work and achievement for a whole course. Self-evaluation might best be carried out, at least in the early stages, by asking yourself specific questions about such things as your purposes, planning and preparation, relationship with the group, your handling of the content and the methods you use, the ways you assess learning outcomes, and so on. Subsequently you may wish to concentrate on one or two aspects in turn.

Some examples of appropriate questions are given below but they are by no means exhaustive. In fact the questions themselves are less important than is the habit of thinking about your work as a teacher of adults, thus both confirming your good practice and modifying those aspects that may require some change.

1   – *Do I respect my students as adults and meet them on equal terms?*
  – *Do I create a friendly, informal and welcoming atmosphere, treating each student as an individual and using his/her name?*
  – *Do I make it apparent that I have time for people, especially before and after a session for those who do not like to speak in front of others or who may want to discuss a private matter?*

2   – *Am I clear about the aims and objectives for the session and have my planning and preparation taken full account of them?*
  – *Do my students know what they are trying to achieve at any given point ... are their needs being met?*
  – *Who sets the standards they are expected to reach? When I do, is it clear to them at what level they have to achieve?*

3 — *Do I show a sufficient willingness to negotiate as well as consult with the group, especially about content?*

— *Do I know my material sufficiently well and have I thought through the order and structure of what I propose to do?*

— *Do I present material step-by-step in short units ... relate new content and ideas to what they already know using appropriate examples ... summarising often?*

4 — *Do people feel confident and at ease within the group ... how do I know? ... what have I done to promote it?*

— *Do I encourage them to contribute their experience and expertise, valuing what they offer, yet sensitively challenging any errors or misapprehensions?*

— *Does everyone get the opportunity to participate and express their opinions, or just the more articulate and able ones?*

5 — *Do I use a range of teaching and learning methods ... and have frequent changes of activities during the session?*

— *Do I use audio visual aids and other learning resources when and where they will help people's learning?*

— *Do I make a task quite clear to people, then sensitively monitor what they are doing ... and, by making use of it subsequently, value it?*

6 — *Am I fair in allocating my time and attention to individuals, especially when they are working on their own?*

— *Can I diagnose and assess people's individual difficulties and, once knowing what they are, can I help individuals in a sympathetic and constructive way?*

— *When I leave an individual does s/he feel satisfied with our discussion ... and know what to do next ... and be motivated to do it?*

7 — *Do I give the group an opportunity to say what they think about the session and the course ... do I listen?*

— *Am I clear about what has been achieved during a session and the extent to which the session's learning objectives have been attained?*

— *Do I ensure that the group and individuals leave with a sense of having accomplished something and a desire to learn more?*

8 – *Do I demonstrate an enthusiasm for my subject, my teaching and my students?*
   – *Are the people in my group motivated, responsive, confident, hard working and full of initiative?*
   – *Do I always remember that it is the learning and achievement of my students that are all important, not my teaching?*

9 – *Do I enjoy what I do and do I do it well? If not, what am I going to do about it?*

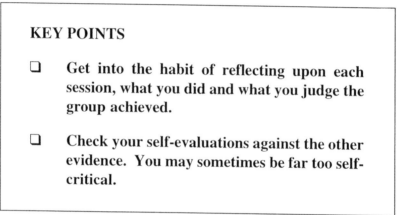

KEY POINTS

❑ **Get into the habit of reflecting upon each session, what you did and what you judge the group achieved.**

❑ **Check your self-evaluations against the other evidence. You may sometimes be far too self-critical.**

21   Student assessment

Assessment involves the sampling of some aspect of a person's behaviour at a particular moment. Depending upon the kind of sample taken, inferences can be drawn about that person's achievements, abilities, motivation, aptitudes and so on. These inferences can in turn be used in a number of ways: to diagnose a student's strengths and weaknesses, to provide him/her with feedback about how s/he is doing, to sustain a sense of motivation and interest, and to provide a formal recognition of accomplishment or competence. Assessment will indicate to the tutor whether specified learning objectives have been achieved, and provide further evidence about the strengths and shortcomings of the course.

Where assessment is used to identify areas of strengths and weaknesses, potential ability or aptitude, it is described as diagnostic; where assessment takes place during a learning sequence and is used to provide feedback to the student about how s/he is doing and progressing towards a desired end, it is described as formative; where assessment is used to measure the extent of the learning that has taken place at the end of a sequence, it is described as summative.

How you actually make assessments of student learning can range from the most informal to the highly formal — from watching and listening to students as they work in the classroom to a set piece examination or assessment of competence. The important features are what it tells you and the student, and how both of you then make use of the information.

1   As you work with a group of adults, you are likely to be making constant, rather intuitive, judgments about the effects of what you are doing. Thus you may identify at a given point in a session that most students seem to have grasped the idea and that you can move on or that few seem able to handle the materials competently and you must stop and give them more practice. This is an appropriate and very desirable set of monitoring and evaluation skills, providing you as the teacher with the feedback you need to decide what you should be doing from one section to the next. Yet whilst you are forming these overall judgments, you will also be aware that a particular student is not coping too well and that another seems way ahead. Perhaps the inferences that tutors draw about some of the more noticeable individuals in a group provides the 'aggregate' feedback about the whole

group. Whether or not this is the case, you do need to ensure that your 'generalised' assessment is fully supplemented by a specific assessment of every individual. You need to know what each member of the group can or cannot do and the extent to which they have met the learning objectives, so that you can offer him/her the right help or guidance.

2 There is much to be said for taking an indirect approach to assessment, making it an integral and everyday aspect of your teaching. Assessment should not appear as anything out of the ordinary, nor should it raise any unnecessary anxiety in your students. You are not so much testing them to find out what they do not know as continually monitoring their progress and achievement, using this feedback to guide their learning and your teaching. Where you do have to undertake more formalised, summative assessment that will assume a higher profile, you should still try to be make it as natural a part of the learning/teaching process as possible.

3 Whatever type of assessment procedure you use, you need to be particularly sensitive to people's feelings and reactions. Adult students may well lack confidence in themselves as learners and too public a demonstration of achievement and especially failure, will not be welcomed, even within the safe confines of the group. Many, for example, would find it rather invidious to be asked to put up a hand if they know the answer or come out to the front to demonstrate to the rest how good they are. They will have vivid memories of similar procedures from their schooling and their expectations now are that they should be treated as adults and not as children.

It is equally important that when you offer formative feedback, you strike a balance between honesty and objectivity on the one hand and a recognition of an individual's potential level of achievement and his/her sensibilities on the other. Your students will have a fair idea of what they are able to do and will welcome some external confirmation, but too much criticism, even where you intend it to be constructive, may be difficult for them to cope with.

4 Identify and use a range of techniques appropriate to your subject which will tell you and your students about their achievements without 'putting them on the spot'. Here are some suggestions:

* You may not actually need a specially designed assessment procedure at all. If you watch how people are working and listen to how they talk to you and to each other, you may have much of the evidence you require. You may well be able to observe whether they are moving in the right way ... handling tools correctly ... using the correct part of speech ... expressing an informed opinion, without doing anything further.

* You could design a task or an activity which, whilst similar to that which they have just been working on, is sufficiently different to allow you to identify whether they can transfer what they have learnt to a different but allied situation.

* With the intention of carefully observing the outcomes, you could:

 — ask people to work together and give each other feedback
 — ask them to work together and prepare a simple routine to show to others
 — give them a case study to see if they can identify the salient points
 — get them to carry out a problem-solving task
 — ask them to draw up some guidelines for someone just starting out
 — get them to role-play a situation in small groups so they can learn from each other
 — prepare some task or activity which, though plainly intended for you and them to find out how they are doing, still retains the element of enjoyment and poses little threat. Thus: a word search sheet; a simple simulation; a game such as *Fill in the Blanks ... Complete the Diagram ... Spot the Mistakes*
 — set a piece of homework where they have to apply what has been learnt and report back. It does not have to involve reading and writing; they could make a short audio tape ... work on a set of newspaper clippings ... review a TV programme ... interview someone ... do a simple experiment ... carry out a short social survey of friends or family.

5 You may well want to ask people questions, seemingly the most obvious way of finding out what they know or think they know. If you do, be sure you know what type of question you are asking and whether the answer will provide you with the sort of evidence you are seeking. (See *Chapter 16: Asking questions.*)

6   There will be occasions when more formal procedures are called for. You may need to check people's understanding, skill and progress before they undertake a field trip, exhibit or perform in public, take an outside examination or move to a more advanced group. You will know the techniques common to your particular subject area, but regardless of the format, you should discuss the procedure with the group and negotiate as much of it with them as you can. Make sure they understand why you are suggesting they attempt it, agree the way that the results are to be handled and fed back to individuals, and respect the right of any member of the group to opt out if s/he wishes, without ridicule or recrimination. Once individuals are fully aware of the purposes of the assessment, the procedure and consequences of taking or not taking part, the choice should still remain theirs.

The same procedure should ideally apply to any formal summative procedure to the extent that it can be, whether it be a public examination, a flower show, a competition, a performance or an end of course display. Students should negotiate the ground rules as far as possible and individuals must decide whether or not they are going to enter. The particular circumstances of the assessment of competences (and of NVQs) are described in the next chapter (*22: Assessing Learning Outcomes*).

7   You have the advantage in a one-to-one situation of being able to find out what the student thinks about his/her achievement. You can ask more direct questions aimed at uncovering particular strengths and weaknesses. You can discover whether s/he fully understands a particular point, or if s/he feels confident about performing a particular skill before asking for a demonstration. However, the need for sensitivity remains paramount. The conversational approach will encourage both of you to greater candour, and whilst the positive feedback and encouragement you offer may result in significant improvement, a casual comment or careless criticism could prove devastating to some individuals.

8   Here are some suggestions for making informal assessments on a one-to-one basis:

   – give the student your full attention
   – remember to use her/his name
   – make eye-to-eye contact, smile and look friendly
   – take care that your discussion is as private as it can reasonably be

- find out what the student thinks about her/his achievement first
- confirm positive self-evaluations but do not collude with self-deprecations unless they are accurate
- reinforce positive aspects
- restrict your criticism of any shortcomings
- use language that will be understood
- relate your assessment to the individual's previous work, rather than to that of other individuals in the group
- discuss with the student what s/he should do next rather than tell him/her
- be specific in any guidance or advice you provide
- ensure that the expectations agreed between the two of you are achievable
- clarify the one or two features that the student is to work at next
- leave on a positive note and thank the student
- find an opportunity to reassess and give further feedback.

9 Students should be encouraged to form opinions about their work and to learn to trust their own judgments. Talking with them on a one-to-one basis about their achievements is one way of helping them develop the skills of self-evaluation. In fact all forms of assessment should include an account of people's self-evaluations; you should build in opportunities for people to reflect upon how they are doing and what they feel about it. They can then compare their views against more 'objective' opinions of their learning and progress. The more practice they have in making judgments of their own work against the 'yardsticks' you can provide as the teacher, the better they will be able to assess their own achievements when they are working entirely on their own.

KEY POINTS

❑ **Assess your students' progress and achievements continuously so that you can identify with them both how they are doing and what is to be done next.**

❑ **First find out what the student thinks about what s/he has done and then offer your judgements in sensitive and constructive ways.**

22   Assessing learning outcomes

In the wider context of education, training and employment, there has been a radical shift in the manner in which formal assessment is carried out. Part of the driving force has been the Government's concern to provide a trained/retrained adult workforce possessing readily transferable qualifications. A further contribution has come from a longstanding debate between individual employer and professional groups on the one hand and educational institutions on the other about the adequacy of training for the workplace. A third factor has been a concern by educators and by learners themselves for a more user-friendly system which focuses on individual needs rather than institutional demands, one moreover which eases transferability of learning 'credit'. In the event, major change has taken place, the most important aspect of which has been a lessening of concern about the content and the process of learning and a much greater interest in the outcomes of learning and their assessment.

1 'Learning outcomes' have the potential to describe changes in an adult learner in two distinct ways. Firstly there are subject-based learning outcomes — knowledge, understanding and skills, the ability to apply such knowledge and understanding (and skills) in different situations and the (mainly) intellectual 'processing skills' that are acquired through using and applying knowledge. Secondly, there are personal learning outcomes — motivation, initiative and self-evaluation ... and interpersonal skills such as negotiation, collaboration and teamwork. Together, they form a much more complete picture of an individual — of greater value to him/herself, to the provider of education and training, to employers and to the community as a whole.

2 Whilst adult educators are uneasy about some of the developments which have taken place, there is much that accords with the principles of adult education. A concern with learning outcomes focuses directly on the adult learner. Much greater account is taken of what learners can do and their individual successes are described in more precise ways. There is greater emphasis on the standards against which learning is assessed. This contrasts with traditional formal assessment procedures which predominantly test learners' knowledge rather than the application of knowledge or its practical use, and then only of selected topics drawn from a course syllabus. In these procedures, learner 'success' is

typically described in terms of being *better* or *worse* than a group of peers.

3   In general, a 'learning outcomes' approach to assessment improves the quality of individual choice, recognises existing learning more efficiently and facilitates transfer from one learning opportunity to another. Most critically it provides evidence of qualification for employment purposes. In the long term a learner-centred system is likely to produce more independent, self-motivated learners than the traditional system with its emphasis on teaching processes, courses and institutional delivery. Learners have greater control of the system and the deliverers — teachers, institutions and awarding bodies — have rather less.

4   A learning outcomes approach to assessment is also of considerable value to tutors (and to managers) too, since it offers a means of measuring individual change which is not just related to the planned curriculum. This is particularly important in adult education where personal as well subject-based outcomes are often highly valued but rarely precisely defined or formally assessed. The development of performance indicators and the increasing need to demonstrate 'value for money' make it important that these outcomes should be clearly defined in order that they continue to be valued.

5   Within the area of vocational education and training the present decade has seen the extensive development of one particular learning outcome — **'competence'**. The term is specific to that learning outcome which is primarily concerned with doing. Though 'competence' embraces both specific task skills and the understanding, knowledge, attitudes and personal skills required to carry out a task effectively, performance is central to the concept. Competence describes the outcomes of the learning process not the process itself. It has to do with the assessment of what has been acquired, not its acquisition. Seen in the context of a course or session, competence is a stage beyond learning objectives; it is a way of measuring what has actually been achieved, rather than what is expected and planned for by the tutor.

6   Assessment of competence requires the demonstration of a particular piece of behaviour and normally involves some supplementary evidence about the knowledge which relates to its use or application. The

process involves an assessor obtaining sufficient evidence of a learner's practical 'capability' and judging whether it has reached an objective, predetermined standard. It requires a statement of context specifying under what circumstances the activity has taken place and the range of other, allied situations in which it would apply. It provides a measure of what someone can do at a particular time, though it does not say that an individual will necessarily continue to be competent, or that s/he will become more competent or that if s/he is not competent that s/he may not become so in the future.

7　'Being competent' means performing to professional and/or occupational standards. An individual who is 'competent' has demonstrated that s/he can actually do 'x' or 'y' to an appropriate, nationally accepted standard. A claim of 'capability' through some overall success on a course where 'x' or 'y' was taught is now deemed inappropriate.

8　In 1986 the Government set up the *National Council for Vocational Qualifications (NCVQ)* to 'hallmark' qualifications which meet the needs of employment — *National Vocational Qualifications (NVQ).* Since that time, NCVQ has been the major force in developing ideas about the meaning of competence and about its application in vocational education and training. NCVQ does not itself offer qualifications. NVQs will be administered by *awarding bodies.* The role of NCVQ is to harmonise vocational qualifications by developing a framework which clarifies the relationship between them. In essence, *units* of competencies are clustered together to form NVQs — defined as a group of units which have relevance to a particular occupational employment.

9　There are five *levels* of NVQs ranging from basic skills to those representing the professions. All vocational qualifications will need to be written as a series of competency statements and will have to meet NCVQ approval criteria. Responsibility for defining competence rests with recognised *lead bodies* which should be led by employers working with employees and educational and training advisers.

10　NVQ statements of competence must be set out in a format which has three levels of detail:

　　– *NVQ Title*: the area of competence encompassed by the qualification and its level
　　– *Unit of competence*: a coherent group of elements of competence and

associate performance criteria, all of which form a discrete activity. It is the smallest unit which can be accredited to an individual

– *Element of competence* with its associate *performance criteria*: a description of an action, behaviour or outcome which an individual should be able to demonstrate. Performance criteria themselves are statements against which an assessor judges evidence that an individual can perform the activity specified in an element.

In addition, *range statements* are written to elaborate statements of competence by making explicit the contexts to which the elements and performance criteria apply.

11 Assessment within NVQs is the process of judging (sufficient) evidence against standards of success which are already defined and available to the assessor and to the candidate. The opportunities for assessing performance are generally limited to normal work in a workplace or in a specifically designed competency test. However, assessment of performance will probably also need to be supplemented with assessments of knowledge and understanding.

12 *Accreditation of prior learning (APL)* is the process by which candidates' existing attainment, skills, knowledge or competence is recognised and given credit. It means that students need not undertake additional training in areas where they are already competent. Evidence of prior learning can come from work experience; independent study; courses; and experience from activities other than employment. Individuals need to build up a portfolio of their work experience, training activities and other relevant experiences (certificates, letters of commendation etc.) as evidence that they really can do what they claim to be able to do.

13 The extent to which you as tutor will have direct dealing with NVQs will depend upon the subjects you teach to adults, and the formal training you undertake as a teacher.

* If you teach in a subject area and/or are employed in an institution which is directly concerned with occupational education and training you will find NVQs at the forefront of learner assessment. If you are required to assess student competence, you yourself will need to demonstrate that you are competent to do so. This will require you to be accredited with the appropriate units of competence, currently offered by several awarding bodies (CGLI, RSA, BTech) within the specifications of the TDLB (Training and Development Lead Body). You will need to be further accredited if you are also involved in verifying the assessment procedures of colleagues and/or formally assessing the prior learning of students.

* If you undertake teacher training leading to certification by one of the awarding bodies (eg C&G 730 course for teachers in further and adult education) your assessment is likely to be competence-based and may well include the TDLB assessor units of competence mentioned above.

* You will find that competency based assessment is time consuming for both candidate and assessor. Where you act as a course tutor and as an assessor you will need to plan your sessions in ways that allow your students to collect and demonstrate their competence and give you the time and space to weigh the evidence they offer and judge whether it reaches the standard required.

14 You may not be formally involved with NVQs; many areas of adult education not directly connected with occupational training and employment will not demand that you should be. However, you need to be aware of this assessment 'culture' even as it continues to undergo change and development. The students you work with may progress in their studies and seek education and training which does involve NVQs or at least focuses on the assessment of learning outcomes. You need to be in a position to offer them guidance about such progression routes and what they may demand of an individual.

15 Perhaps, most importantly, you need to think about the ways you carry out and document more formal assessments of your students. It is doubtful whether you should be writing your own set of competencies, but you should be looking for ways in which you can assess your students' subject-based and personally-based learning outcomes. Where you do use formal procedures think through the ways in which you can best carry out the process, the nature of the evidence you will consider, the standards you are going to apply and how you are going to record and feed back the results. Your students should keep copies of any assignments plus your assessment comments and should retain them carefully for future use as evidence of 'prior learning and achievement'. To this end, ensure that your feedback comments/reports are sufficiently detailed and specify clearly the standard attained. Any

assessment of learning you undertake should be to provide people with proof of their successful learning and you, incidentally, with evidence about the effectiveness of your teaching.

KEY POINTS

❏   Employ a variety of strategies to assess the learning outcomes of individual students. They may well be different for each though perfectly valid for (and valued by) the person concerned.

❏   Keep abreast of developments in assessment procedures. It is in your students' interests that you should do so.

V Getting Started

23 Constructing session plans

There can be few adult tutors who do not undertake some sort of preparation for their teaching, though each will approach the business of session planning in ways which best suit him/herself. Yet writing out a session plan is only one step in the process of planning for learning. It is the culmination of a period of preparation and planning which can involve reading, reflection, discussion with students, selecting content, choosing appropriate methods, thinking through activities, anticipating group management issues, designing teaching aids, reviewing previous sessions, and so on.

1   It may be helpful to consider the following framework:

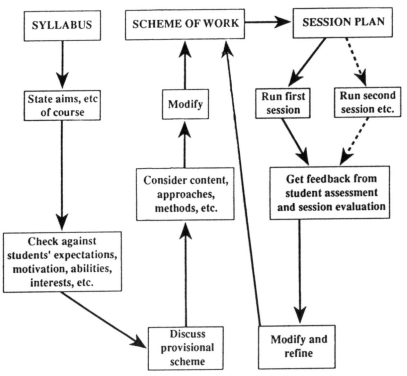

2   Whatever labels you prefer to give to these elements, and however you document them, each has an important part to play in planning for learning.

* A **course syllabus** usually includes a general description of the course — its title, aims, areas of content to be covered, level, group size, staffing, resources, timing, place and venue. It is not simply an itemised list of course content. By writing it at an early stage and clarifying these issues you will be in a much better position to decide how the course is to be organised.

* A **scheme of work** sets out session by session the work which it is anticipated will be covered and how it will be approached. Does the subject   demand a certain order — are there fundamental principles or skills that have to be tackled before anything else or can some things be safely left until later? What might people enjoy doing at the beginning of the course that will give them a sense of achievement and a desire for more? What major learning/ teaching methodologies are to be employed, when might they best be used them and are there any practical constraints of resources which need to be taken into account? How are ongoing course evaluation and student assessments to be undertaken? Setting out these considerations into a working programme or scheme of work will allow you to see the overall structure of what you are proposing to do.

* A **session plan** provides a relatively detailed working plan of a session set out in a format which the individual teacher finds most useful. It usually includes some indication of the purposes of the session (its aims and objectives), some reference to the proposed subject content, the teaching/learning methods to be used, timing, materials and resources, plus a note about the student assessment techniques and session evaluation procedures to be used. Few adult teachers venture very far without such *aide -mémoires* even if some still call it *a lesson plan*, a term reminiscent of schooling rather than adult work. You will find such plans invaluable.

3   It will be apparent that the relationship between these three descriptions is not only one of level — from the general to the specific — but also a dynamic one. It will be an unusual adult session where everything goes perfectly to plan. Most tutors find that they have to adapt a session as it proceeds, taking into account unforeseen circumstances, modifying over-ambitious or too simplistic-plans and adapt-

ing to the pace of participants' learning. In this way, the outcomes of one session can and should influence the planning and conduct of the next and, in turn, modify the scheme of work.

4 Most of us do not plan in a very logical fashion. We may have a rough idea of what we might do and what we want students to attempt, some thoughts about an appropriate visual aid, a wish to use a particular method, a need to reinforce an item not understood too well in a previous session, a desire to move on to a new area of interest, and so on. These elements take time to coalesce into a viable learning event and the chances are that most tutors make several attempts at designing a particular session.

5 The session plan itself is a teacher's practical working document. Experienced tutors usually include some of the following in their session plans. You should select those items which will be of value to you and add any others that you think would be useful:

 − Date of session
 − Duration
 − Venue and room
 − Type of group (description; may include some indication of previous knowledge)
 − Number in group (may include a list of participants and/or seating plan)
 − Topic
 − Aim and objectives (may be defined as 'overall and specific purposes')
 − Resources
 − Arrangement of the environment
 − Session 'structure' showing timing, content and methods
 − Evaluation (student achievements and course evaluation)
 − Note of 'what to do next'
 − Note of 'what to modify if this session is repeated'.

6 There is no single formulation, no 'best way' to set out session plans. Some possibilities include:

 − a timed sequence of notes of what is to be done
 − a table with column heading: *timing + objectives + content + methods + aids*
 − a table with column headings: *what the students are to do and why + what I am to do + what with + when*

- a flow diagram: boxes and arrows showing *what -> how -> when* graphically.

Whichever format you decide on, leave space to write in what happened during the session. Make a note of anything that went particularly well ... and less well; indicate anything that you would change another time and what you need to do next time. Do not delay doing it, thinking you will remember later: you will not, and your insight as well as your good ideas may be lost.

7   Some practical tips:

- make the critical points stand off the page in some way: use highlighter pens, underline or write things in different coloured inks
- keep all your session plans for a particular course sequentially in a binder file
- if you find you need reference notes about a piece of content, detailed factual material that you cannot carry in your head, write them down separately. Use different coloured paper so it is obvious to you which is which. Some tutors like to use record cards: if you do, number them in case you drop them or, better still, punch a hole in one corner and tie them together with a loop of string or a treasury tag
- keep a copy of every handout you plan to use with your session plans. Write any management instructions that you want to remember on it clearly. (Keep the master sheet of any handouts you intend to use in a thin transparent plastic folder and place it in the back of the course binder. You may need more copies!)
- place any prepared A4 OHP acetate sheets in plastic folders with a layer of thin plain paper between each. If you are using mounted OHP acetates, label and number them clearly.

8   Realistically, you should not expect that all your session or course aims and objectives will be achieved just because you planned carefully at the beginning. Planning for learning requires a flexible approach, continual modification and adaption. It demands that, as teachers, we take full account of the ongoing needs and learning achievements of the people we work with. Since they are adults, we are in the fortunate position of being able to share this process with them, consulting and negotiating with them about the most appropriate ways forward.

KEY POINTS

❑ Take time and trouble in any planning for learning you undertake; it will result in better teaching and more effective learning.

❑ Strike a balance between what people need, what they have already achieved and the learning opportunities you can realistically provide for them.

24   The first session

What a tutor does within the first few minutes of a session, whether the session is the first in a sequence or a 'one off' event, will critically affect what happens thereafter.

1   Essentially, an effective beginning has to do with:

   – gaining people's attention and creating an interest in what is to follow
   – helping people settle down, relax and feel at ease with one another and the tutor
   – setting the expectation and tone for the rest of the session (and of the course)
   – establishing a climate conducive to learning and achievement.

The last few minutes of a session are a crucial time for:

   – helping people consolidate and value what they have achieved
   – motivating people to continue with their learning
   – finding out what participants think about the session and what was attempted
   – 'trailing' a subsequent session.

2   The first session with any new group of adults is a testing occasion for new and experienced tutors alike. Unless course members have worked together before or have met each other previously, they are likely to lack confidence in themselves, feel ill at ease in the company of other participants and may even be doubting the wisdom of having joined the course. There is nothing surprising about this anxiety and it is to be expected. However, it is crucial that students should quickly feel at ease and ready to learn; they will, quite rightly, look to the tutor to aid this process. Some of the strategies which may help you get things right first time are listed below.

3   Arrive in plenty of time and make yourself known to the staff member on duty, the office staff and the caretakers. Find out their names and use them. Administrative staff and caretakers are critical people in any educational establishment; you can be sure you will have need of their help and support!

* Locate the resources store, the photocopier and so on and find out the normal procedures for using them.

* Establish if and when refreshments are available and where the nearest lavatories are to your teaching room so that you can give this information to the group. Identify where the emergency exits are.

* Check there are no last minute room or timetable changes, administrative requests, or alterations in the enrolment procedures.

Most of this preparatory work is better done on a short preliminary visit some days before. You will then feel much more at ease as you arrive for a first session since you already know where you are going, what it is like and what you have to contend with.

4 Inspect your teaching room, and if materials have been left out by previous occupants, tidy them away as far as you are able. Draw yourself a quick sketch of the room so that you can put everything back where you found it at the end of the session.

* If the room is not suitably arranged for the sort of work you are going to do, change it. Try to avoid straight rows of chairs and tables; a circle or U shape is likely to be better. Tables may not be needed at all, though some people may initially prefer the security of sitting behind desks. If you need a table to work from then place your chair to the side rather than behind. Even if the group are to be physically active throughout the session, place chairs round the work area so that they have somewhere to sit, especially when they first arrive. Match the number of chairs (and work stations) to the expected number in the group. If you know that one or more of your students has some disability, be ready to adapt the layout appropriately once you know what s/he prefers. Adjust the heating, lighting and ventilation as necessary.

* Check that all the equipment you need is there, that you know how to use it and that it works. Position it in such a way that everyone will be able to see and hear. If you need to use a piece of equipment later in the session, mark its positioning with chalk on the floor or table and put it to one side in an easily accessible place. Lay out your materials and notes in order so that they are available when you need them. Clean the board, put a fresh sheet of paper on the flip chart and wipe

the lenses on the overhead projector. Put a simple hand lettered sign giving the session or course title on the outside of the door. Have your teaching box to hand!

* When you have finished your preparation, check round the room to see that it looks neat, purposeful and welcoming. It sets the tone of your session and people will notice the results of your efforts as soon as they come in.

5 Since you will be fully prepared and ready to go before anyone arrives, you are free to acknowledge and greet individuals. Introduce yourself to each one as s/he comes in and do not be afraid to smile! If you have an enrolment list, familiarise yourself with participants' names and use them. Listen to what people say — they may give you some further clues about themselves and their interests. Introduce people to one another so that they can chat together. Ensure you are not button-holed by an over-talkative individual at the expense of other new arrivals.

* Prepare a set of name badges beforehand. On this first occasions you will have to decide what names you are going to use, though for most adult education settings first names are appropriate. Use a dark, permanent ink felt-tipped pen and write in print large enough for you to be able to read each label at a distance. Wear one yourself and hand them out as people arrive, with a request that they be worn straight away. Have some spares ready for those who prefer a different name. If you do not have a name list, ask people what they would like to be known as and write badges for them; if people write their own, ensure they use a thick pen and they write in large letters. You might also prepare table name plates by folding index cards; write the names on both sides so that others sitting alongside can see who their close neighbours are.

* Some people are reluctant to wear badges, but if you explain that it is predominantly for your benefit so that you can learn their names, few are likely to refuse. It is a good idea to ask the group to leave their badges with you at the end of the session. You are more likely to remember them next time than they are!

6 When the majority of people have arrived — and certainly no later than five minutes beyond the starting time — you should begin.

* Your physical position in relation to the group is important in helping to gain their attention and communicating with them. Some tutors prefer to stand; others feel more comfortable sitting down. One or two even kneel! There are no hard and fast rules, but remember to make sure that everyone can see and hear you and that you in turn can see and hear each student.

* Your choice of words and the manner in which you begin are important. Sound friendly and welcoming, and give the impression of being quietly confident and enthusiastic. Maintain direct eye contact with people and speak clearly at a suitable pace. Try to use a natural, fluid eye movement so that you include each member of the group in what you are saying.

* Announce that you are wanting to start but wait until you have everyone's attention. Greet the group and thank them for coming promptly. Introduce yourself by name and say something about yourself and your interest in the course topic.

7   Some tutors like to start a session with *ice breakers*. They feel that these social group techniques promote the integration of individuals and help a group to 'gel'. This may well be true when students have experienced such methods before and feel at ease with them. They do have an important part to play in sessions concerned with experiential topics such as Human Relations where they serve to begin the process of building trust. However, many adults, especially those new to adult education, may be rather startled by their use and some may be distinctly alienated, especially when they have been given no prior warning. Unless you feel quite confident that all the circumstances are right, it may be wise to avoid the more lengthy or extravagant games.

8   Nevertheless, it is a good idea for people to begin to get to know about each other. One useful procedure, especially for larger groups, is for the tutor to pose general questions about previous experience, background and so on and ask for a show of hands. Another non-threatening method for smaller groups is to ask people to say who they are, where they come from plus one (or two) things about their interest in the subject. This can be done first in pairs or small groups and then relayed to the large group by the individual or by his/her partner. You could draw yourself a simple seating plan as they report back and make a note of who is interested in what.

9 It is at this point in the session that a choice has to be made: to get started on the initial phase of the course content, or to deal with administrative and organisational items. There is a need to do both at some stage, but the decision about the order will depend upon the course content, the tutor and the nature of the group. Some vital issues must be dealt with straight away — emergency exits, workshop safety, break and finishing times, but the majority could quite reasonably be left until the session is underway.

There is much to be said for beginning the course proper as soon as possible and engaging people with some subject content. This is why they have come. Make the opening colourful and lively. Use an aid, a personal anecdote, a story from a student or a classic 'chestnut' drawn from your subject to focus people's attention. An imaginative and brisk opening helps create interest and motivate people. Then if you can, employ a non-threatening and enjoyable method which will allow the group to actively participate together. In the process they will learn something, be able to recognise that they have done so, and begin to get to know each other. Consultation and discussion about your proposals for the course — the syllabus, course content, teaching/learning methods, student assignments — can be undertaken more realistically once group participants feel that they have already begun the process. They will be more willing to articulate their expectations of themselves, of the course, and of the tutor as a result.

10 Administrative and organisational matters must not be neglected, however, even if some items are intentionally left until a subsequent session. Some of the issues which may need to be considered include:
   – health and safety information/drills
   – institutional requirements
   – registers and registration
   – appointing a group representative
   – session cancellation arrangements
   – fees
   – other necessary student expenditure
   – course materials
   – special clothing or dress
   – resource sharing arrangements
   – external examination requirements
   – certification
   – session times and timing

- breaks and coffee time
- smoking
- travel sharing arrangements
- parking

Some of these items are matters of information whilst others can more appropriately be dealt with in consultation with the group.

11 Towards the end of the session take time to discover what they think about what you have done together and what they feel they have learnt. Value their comments and let it be seen that you will give each one due consideration.

* Summarise what you think has been covered and what you judge has been achieved; say something about the standard of what has been attained.

* Confirm any formal arrangements which have been agreed regarding the procedure and organisation of subsequent sessions. Say what you hope will be covered in the next session, accentuating the potentially enjoyable and rewarding features. Remind them of anything they have to do or bring for next time.

* Make it easy for individuals to clarify any general queries that they may have about the course, though suggest that they may prefer to reserve any questions of a personal nature until afterwards.

* Thank them for their interest and attendance, and indicate that you have enjoyed working with them and look forward to seeing them again next time.

12 Get into the habit of being 'first in, last out', not just at a first session but at all of them. Staying behind gives you the opportunity to pack away your materials and resources and to ensure that the room gets put back to its original layout. More importantly, it gives individual group members the space to speak to you on their own or in small groups. This is especially important at the end of a first session. At this stage people might have a variety of issues that they may want your guidance or opinion about which they feel are inappropriate to bring up in front of the group. They may want to confide in you, be reassured that they can cope, or tell you that they will have to miss a future session. You will thus learn a great deal about individuals,

their progress and their problems and at the same time gain valuable feedback about your teaching and management. Be ready to listen. Once everyone has left, you are free to think about the session and how it went and what you need to do for next time.

13 Much of what has been written above is equally applicable to 'one-off' sessions but there are differences in emphasis that are worth noting. A 'one-off' event typically takes place with an unknown group as far as the tutor is concerned, though the participants may be an established group working with another tutor on other occasions.

14 There are some advantages connected with teaching an already established group. The participants will have established a sense of group identity; there will be a shared 'course culture' and people will be aware of their own expectations and the extent to which they are being met. They can be expected to be familiar with the environment in which you will be working together. Other people will have acted as tutors and/or administrators for the group and they will be able to provide you with useful information about the students and the setting. Take care, however, not to be over-influenced by their subjective judgment. Where it is feasible, try to meet the group beforehand and establish directly with them what might be done and how. Simply being introduced to group members informally can provide a point of contact which will make meeting them on the day easier.

15 A major difficulty for you as a visiting tutor will be to establish your credibility and style with the group on their territory. Problems can arise where previous tutors have been poor and the group may have a low expectation of course staff and of themselves. On the other hand, the quality of tutoring may have been first class, in which case you will have a demanding standard to maintain. Above all you should be clear about what is expected of you and the proposed objectives of your session.

* It is particularly important that you are fully prepared right from the start. A visit to the venue beforehand will prove of considerable value to you in your planning: you will have a much better idea of what is possible on the day. As before, you should get there early and take time to set up the teaching space; bear in mind any layout the group may have been used to. There is no reason why you should not greet people as they arrive even though they may feel it is their room; it will

help you to make personal contact with individuals before you start the session. Ask them to wear name badges for your benefit.

* The first few minutes of a one-off session are critical. You need to establish your credentials and competence as a tutor whilst at the same time acknowledging the group's prior existence and shared experience. Since individuals know each other, they are likely to be relatively forthcoming and your asking for particular people's identity or background should not be threatening. (Remember, however, that what they say may only be new to you.) Whatever procedure you use, your purpose is to explore the group's knowledge and experience and to identify points of contact between their skills and knowledge and what you are proposing to do with with them.

16 On those occasions when you are working with a 'once-only' group recruited for just one session, remember that the members of the group will probably not know each other and the total number attending will be uncertain.

17 At the end of any type of 'one-off' session, undertake some type of evaluation in addition to the informal observation you will have done during the session. How has the session gone and what do people feel they have achieved? Offer the group your evaluation.

* Confirm any undertaking you have made about follow-up materials and remind them of any activity that they have agreed to carry out. Indicate the avenues that individuals might pursue to develop the work you have been doing with them.

* Thank them for allowing you to join them and say how you have enjoyed the experience. Do not disappear too quickly; give people space to talk with you on their own. They might just want to say something nice about the session and to thank you.

* Review the session later, taking into account both the group's evaluation and your own. Write a note to the tutor or host and tell him/her how the session went. Include a word of thanks to the group and ask that it be passed on if that is feasible.

KEY POINTS

❑ How you present and manage the first few minutes of a session will set the tone of what is to follow.

❑ How you end a session and talk with people afterwards can powerfully affect their motivation to achieve and to continue learning.

25   Working with large groups

Teaching large groups of 50+ calls for some changes in emphasis and modification of approach rather than a new set of skills, since the same key principles of adult learning and teaching apply here as elsewhere. Many of the strategies and techniques which are successful with smaller groups can work as well with larger ones, though careful planning and confident management are needed. Understandably, the size of the group and of the room can seem daunting at first, but initial nervousness soon dissipates and a good session can become exhilarating.

This last chapter is necessarily an amalgam of many of the ideas and techniques already outlined in this book. As it builds upon a number of particular points made in Chapters 7, 8, 10, 24 and to a lesser extent in Chapter 15, it is suggested that these are reviewed first.

1   **Lecture structure and timing:** The structure of a lecture or talk and the more important aspects of giving explanations are given in Chapter 10. You may like to reconsider the following, however.

* Structure

    – Choose a lecture type to suit the content: a problem-solving approach could be more helpful to listeners than a 'classical structure' or 'sequential structure', and *vice versa* .
    – Structure your talk in a logical sequence: orientation -> key points -> summary. For once, an old chestnut is appropriate: *"say what you are going to say, say it, then say what you've said"*.
    – Build in and use a range of organisers eg signposts, frames, foci links and key points.
    – Tell the group what you hope to cover and how you propose to structure the material — 'x' sections / 'y' points.

* Examples

    – Employ a range of varied examples and analogies.
    – Say the same thing in a different way if an idea is at all difficult. In so doing you are giving further opportunity for people to think about what you have said and see it in relationship to what they already know.

* Timing

  – Begin promptly and *never* go beyond time unless you have explicit permission from everyone to do so.
  – Break up the session eg have 2 x 25 minute sessions + a mid break rather than a 55 minute 'whole'; give mini breaks for shuffles, stretches and coughs!

* 'Other' Presenters

  – Bring in someone else to do a short 'celebrity spot' on his/her speciality. Be sure s/he's fully briefed on what you want done.
  – Employ an actor to simulate a role or injury (use *great circumspection* with a real patient or client — everyone, including the group, must give their consent beforehand).
  – Act out a piece of role-play with a (prepared) stooge — colleague or student. One or two of the audience *might* be willing to replicate it in front of the others, but do not count on it.
  – Use video and sound vignettes of other people acting out a situation, giving their opinions, relating their experiences
  – Record yourself doing 'a piece to camera' in a relevant context and play it back to the group.

* Notes

  – Write out in sequence the notes you feel you need, adding in a simple time plan, the examples you want to give, the A/V aids you are going to use, etc. Underline/highlight the important points. Number the sheets (or record cards) and/or attach them together.
  – Avoid reading from a prepared text; it is always obvious and is rarely done well. If you have no alternative, write it as a radio script to be listened to, not as a journal article to be read.
  – You will probably find that you need make only occasional reference to your notes anyway, given that you have thought through the session in detail and that you have reviewed your notes immediately before the session.

2 **Self-presentation:** What are sometimes called communication skills take on particular importance when working with large groups. You are to be the focus of attention most of the time and, whether you like it or not, your message will be affected not only by how you structure and phrase what you have to say but also how you present it physically — verbally and non-verbally.

* Voice

  - Speak more slowly and enunciate clearly. Use pauses, emphasis and other 'extra verbal' cues to indicate what is important.
  - Project your voice; if a microphone is crucial, use a body microphone to avoid being tied to one spot.

* Gesture and movement

  - Use gestures and movement with verve. They are valuable for communicating with others. Gestures can underline a point, describe an object or action, and illustrate an emotion; movement can add dynamism and interest.
  - Be yourself and do not feel constrained, though avoid semaphore and marathon walks. Control excessive verbal tics — *Er, OK, You know,* as well as obvious nervous mannerisms.
  - Avoid any behaviour which might seriously distract people and get in the way of their learning.

* Positioning

  - Make sure you can be seen by everyone without appearing too dominant. A low dais may help. Alternatively, create an open space between you and the front row.
  - If you have to stand behind a lectern or table, come out from behind it from time to time.
  - If you do need a table, stand or sit to the side. You will appear more open to the audience and you can still lay out your materials. Better still, work in front of it!

* Dress

  - Dress to suit the occasion, the audience and the topic as well as yourself. Inappropriate clothing will detract from your credibility though the unexpected can create attention and interest.

* Manner

  - Strive to appear quietly confident and relaxed. If you are fully prepared and organised then you will appear to be in control.
  - Be seen to be enthusiastic about your subject and about what you are planning to do with the group.
  - Smile and look people in the eyes.
  - Use humour but resist becoming a stand-up comic.

    – Demonstrate in all you say and do that you have a respect for the adulthood and equality of everyone present.

3 **Participatory activities:** The point has already been made in this book that both participation and variety are crucial in aiding the learning process. There is no reason why a range of participatory methods cannot be used with larger groups. Such methods can work remarkably well where their choice and management is given some forethought and they are employed with a degree of confidence. Chapter 10 implies that a 'liquorice allsort sandwich' of tutor + student activities and interaction is preferable to the traditional 'talk+questions-at-the-end'. Some participatory activities that can be built into a session include:

* Voting

    – Ask for 'hands-up' to indicate *Who does what ... who agrees/ disagrees ...who has most/least? etc.*
    – Build in some humorous questions.
    – Give some confection or fruit as prizes to 'winners' of inconsequential items.

* Buzz groups

    – Use them at any time. Monitor what people say to each other and use the results in what you do next.
    – Quick, informal dialogues function as mini breaks.
    – Take the opportunity to reorganise your notes or equipment.

* Brainstorm

    – Ask for single words — take in a sample.
    – It may be helpful to have (a prearranged) person to write them up on a flip chart as you 'stage manage' hearing each one and then repeating them for the group's benefit and for the scribe's. (S/he may not be able to write up each item in the way you want them organised, however).
    – The activity can be fun, especially if you 'ham it up' a bit, though you must value and record everything that is offered.

* Group work (2, 3 or 4s)

    – Tell people to work with the person in the next seat and/or turn round to those behind.

    – Check to see every one has a partner; bring together those who have not.

    – Ensure the task is quite clear to everyone. Use a handout and/or an OHP in addition to explaining verbally what you want them to do.

* Tasks

    - Use a variety of different tasks and activities: solve a problem; read an extract or *précis*; agree a response/answer with a partner; study and respond to photographs or diagram (on a slide/OHP/handout); debate an issue taking sides; role-play a situation; practice a technique; teach each other.

    - Some activities can include an observer who offers feedback to his/her partners (and to you).

    - Repeat any role-based activity so that everyone plays each part in turn.

* Snowballing

    – Start with individuals, then combine in 2s, then 4s.

    – Consider letting it grow to a 'two x half' group vote.

    – Work out the numbers and how many items are to be discarded with each increase in group size (See Chapter 16).

    – It can become chaotic but great fun!

    – The activity provides a break with plenty of welcome movement, though it can be time consuming.

* Rainbowing

    – Ask the initial 2/3/4s to reform with each individual creating a group with entirely new partners.

    – Encourage people to share their previous group's solutions, and then compare, combine and/or develop their ideas further.

    – The sharing which takes place lessens the need for you to take in general feedback from the whole group.

* Large group

    – Invite people to call out their responses/observations/ questions to slides, objects, verbal propositions, etc. Make sure you set the tone for what you have in mind.

    – Direct the group to simulate a phenomena or piece of behaviour eg a wave motion; a DNA molecule; discords and harmonies; speech rhythms; a Greek chorus; a Mexican Wave!

* Questions

  – Negotiate with the group whether questions are to be asked *during* and/or *after* the session. Declare your preference.
  – End-of-session question time can often result in silence, so give time for people to check out a potential question with a partner to confirmed that it is worth asking. (S/he may be able to answer it, too.)
  – Suggest that 'pairs' ask the question: *We would like to know* ...
  – Have them write questions on cards, collect and shuffle them, then answer as many as you have time for.
  – Encourage questions. They will indicate levels of interest, links with other ideas and understanding as well as what learning has taken place.

It was pointed out in Chapter 15 that participatory activities must be monitored, shared and valued. Similar techniques for taking in feedback can be used during a large group 'plenary' session, though they need to be carefully managed and of necessity they will be more perfunctory. You will not be able to hear from every small group — and the audience will recognise you will not be able to do so — but you should sample what people have done. Get the flavour by asking two or three pairs/trios to call out one of their more important responses or ideas and then seek the whole group's confirmation that these represent the general opinion. Ask whether what you heard as you monitored some of the discussions is in fact what most people identified. The management of plenary feedback almost calls for a degree of fairground theatricality. Make it fun and keep it moving even though it has important purposes, not least of which is telling you how much they have learnt.

4 **A/V Hardware:** There are a number of pieces of audio-visual equipment which lend themselves to use with large groups though you should take care that the image (and/or sound) is clear for everyone. Go and check from the back of the room before the session begins. Make use of some of the following:

* Writing boards (white/chalk)

  – Use only black + primary colour dri-marker pens on a white board; ensure you have an eraser and fluid.
  – Use only white or yellow chalk on a chalk board; have a duster to hand.

    – Practise writing large letters in straight lines ... and without any screeching.

    – Wipe the board clean before the session starts.

* Flip chart

    – Use black + primary colour thick pens.

    – Write especially large and keep words to a minimum.

    – *Fix* A1 sheets on the wall with *Blu-Tack* to give more writing space.

    – *Appliqué* shapes, flash cards, symbols etc with *Blu-Tack*.

    – Prepare items beforehand and keep them covered; use jumbo paper clips to hold several sheets together.

    – Trace in the outline of 'spontaneously drawn' items with soft, feint pencil beforehand.

    – Use thick paper and *Blu-Tack* as a revealing technique.

* Magnetic board

    – Use sticky-backed magnetised tape on the back of 'flash cards' and objects. It is an ideal technique for showing movement and alternative rearrangements of items.

    – Make items and any lettering large enough.

    – Have a sharp colour contrast between the background and the edges of 'magnetised' cards.

* *Velcro* surface

    – Use *Marler Haley* display materials (velcro and brushed nylon). It is ideal for building up a chart or flow diagram from pre-prepared items during a talk.

    – Use large, colour-contrasted items and lettering.

    – Set up linked boards as a free standing unit or support a board on the ledge of a flip chart stand.

    – Carry a piece of brushed nylon as an emergency/easy-to-carry-and-then-tack-up screen.

* Overhead projector

    – Ensure that the screen is large enough; consider projecting onto the wall (build a screen from A1 paper and *Blu-Tack*).

    – Avoid shape distortion of the projected image by keeping the screen and the upper OHP lens parallel.

    – Avoid hiding behind it — put it on a reversed chair rather than on a

table or a too-high stand. Mark its position on the floor with chalk for easy repositioning.
- Clean the glass surfaces with a soft cloth.
- Check that it is not too noisy — if it is, replace it.
- Stay out of the illumination; switch it off when its not needed.
- Lay a pen or something similar on the projected acetate as a pointer. If you wish to point to the screen, use a pointer and keep yourself well to the side.

* 35mm Slides

- Severely limit the 'hard data' displayed on any one slide.
- Restrict the number of slides you show in any particular sequence: people soon get fatigued.
- Include human interest items — people, places and objects — they help association and identification with a topic.

* Video (playback)

- View any video film yourself before showing it.
- Restrict total viewing time to less than 20 minutes.
- Prepare your introduction and the group's related task beforehand.
- Set up three (or five) monitors ... one centrally and one(or two) on either side and check them for sound balance. Use a video-projector if there is one.
- Ensure the counter scale is the same as the one you used.
- Check the video recorder and have it set ready to go.
- Lend the tape to people for private viewing afterwards.

* Video camera (CCTV)

- Set up three/five monitors and check the sound levels.
- Brief the operator about exactly what you want him/her to show and/or record.
- Use it to show fine details of demonstrations, models, diagram, replays of a role play, etc, direct to the audience as well as recording your presentation for subsequent viewing.

* Tape recorder

- Listen to all the tape before you use it.
- Prepare your introduction and the group's related task.
- Restrict total listening time to less than 10 minutes.

- Re-record the extracts you want to use on to a new tape.
- Go 'forwards' only. If you need to replay an earlier piece for comparison, record it again ie A -> B -> C ->A.
- Connect the recorder to the lecture room's sound system or obtain an amplifier. No domestic model will be loud enough.
- Show 'blown-up' photographs of speakers during playback.
- Make several copies and lend them out to people afterwards.

* Models

- Ensure that they are large enough. It is very frustrating to the audience if they are too small.
- Use a CCTV to show details.
- Produce and display giant simulations.
- Have plenty of examples if they are to be passed round; expect some disruption and lack of attention as they go from hand to hand.
- Make them available for people to inspect and handle as they leave at the end of the session.

5 **Projections:** The overhead projector is ubiquitous. If you have not used one then you should familiarise yourself with one as soon as possible. It is invaluable for all sizes of group. Transparencies should be prepared beforehand. They can be A4 size, square, permanent or non-permanent, with or without cardboard mounts. Keep them flat at all times and separated by plain paper spacers

* Transparencies (acetates, film or foils)

- They can be hand lettered or stencilled with non permanent/water-soluble or permanent/spirit-based OHP pens.
- Obtain an eraser fluid pen for use with permanent pens.
- Use only black and primary colours 'medium' tipped pens.
- Limit the information per sheet: 7 words on 7 lines, maximum.
- Place a sheet of lined paper underneath as a guide and leave 1.5" at the top and bottom
- Avoid using a continuous roll during a session unless you have an excellent hand. Then only use water soluble pens and write in randomised blocks rather than straight lines.
- They can be 'machine made'. Prepare an original using lettering and line drawings then photocopy onto special 'dry toner' acetates.
- Alternatively, print a computer-designed item directly onto a dry

toner acetate via a laser printer.

- Typewritten script is always too small — 18 pt or 1/4 inch 'bold' is the minimum size you should consider.
- Transparencies can be coloured by hand or with a colour photocopier or with a colour laser printer.

* Overlays

- Combine two or more acetates and hinge them with masking tape.
- Align correctly by drawing *after* hinging; enhance them with colour.

* Strips

- Cut 'boxed' items from a prepared transparency into strips etc; display them as you speak to each one.
- Make a transparency of a supermarket trolley, basket or other container to use as a visual 'receptacle'.

* Silhouette

- Use coins, cut out card shapes, etc, to produce novel arrangements and to show movement.
- Float items on a little liquid in a flat, glass dish *but take great care of the electrical safety aspect if the OHP is underlit.*

6 **Note taking:** Many adults will feel they ought to be taking notes and some will actively want to do so. A few will know from past experience that writing notes as they listen helps them structure the information and understand it better. Everyone should feel free to make notes if they wish to, though most might find it more useful in the long run to listen and participate in the session with you providing the 'gist' in a handout at the end. Consider the following:

* Verbatim note taking

- Discourage it. Unless they are taken in good shorthand such notes are always inaccurate. Writers hardly engage with the material and remember little of what they hear.

* Analytical note taking

- Encourage people to listen and then note down only the major points and critical examples in a structured way.

- Help people recognise the important points by your lecture structure tactics (foci, signposts etc) and the extra-verbal markers you use (stress, pauses, etc).
- Make some sample notes and display them on the OHP to give them the idea. Alternatively, give out a first 10 minutes' worth of notes of the session as a 'starter' handout.

* Summary note writing

   - 'Forbid' note taking, then give 5 minutes in every 15+ minutes for people to put them together, working individually or collaboratively.
   - Allow them to check with a partner and/or your summary OHP.
   - This procedure will promote people's analysis, understanding and retention of the ideas and material.

* Skeletal

   - Provide outline notes with spaces on a handout to be completed by note-taking students during the session (See 7 below).

* Collaborative

   - Suggest that pairs take notes *one on/one off* over agreed 10/15 minute note taking spell, using carbons or photocopying afterwards.
   - Allow time for partners to agree format and style before you start.

* Tape recording

   - Allow anyone to tape record the session.
   - Do the same yourself and lend the tape to anyone who wants it, (including any absentees).
   - Listen to it yourself and use it to evaluate your presentation. (Do the same for any video recording you might make.)

* Your notes

   - Offer photocopies of your lecture notes for those who would like to work from them. Why not?

7 **Handouts:** People have come to expect handout material. If you cannot get free photocopying, 'hide' the cost in the overall fee. If you have to charge, make sure that people are willing to pay and undertake to produce only 'value for money' copies. (Use a 72% reduction and

double the quantity of printing on an A4 sheet; propose that friends might like to share copies and cost).

Take time and trouble to produce good quality handouts as they reflect directly upon your professionalism. Use the same type face and layout for each one; design a unique heading for the particular group and print it as the top inch or so of each handout; if you are reproducing a page from a book, remove any dirty edge-lines and irrelevant text, then centre and remount it on plain paper before copying; 'spot' dirty master sheets with *Tipp-Ex*. Do not put any reference-dates on your handout masters — if you reprint them for another occasion, an old date will be commented on adversely.

Groups of all sizes seem unable to pass round even a single pile of handouts without confusion. Walk back and pass enough along each row, though you might give some out personally to the people you can reach. Retrieve any spares straight away. Do not start a second set until the first is well under way. Check everyone has everything before you continue. Better still, make up individual sets of coloured (or large-numbered) handouts and put them in A4 envelopes. Give them out at the start and ask people to take items out as you tell them (Those who are colour blind can work with a partner). Give handouts to friends for any absentee or put aside a named set for them.

You could use some of the following:

* Skeletal

    – Set out the major points and leave gaps for people to add to during a session.
    – Draw a diagrammatic boxed layout to be filled in as you talk.

* Summary

    – Include all the important points and examples, akin to a first class set of student notes.

* Task

    – Specify the task or activity you want people to undertake. Suggest they *Make some notes below.*

* Articles

    – Reproduce an (edited) article or a summary-précis. Give the full reference.

— Photocopy a couple of complete texts for those who would like to borrow them after the session.

* Reading list

— Construct a realistic, user-friendly and annotated reading list.
— Say where books can be found. Give the library reference codes; identify likely bookshops and prices.
— Provide some notes on the main areas covered by each.
— Indicate the 'quality' and importance of texts (eg * /**/***).

* Diagrams

— Reproduce unlabelled or part-labelled graphics to be filled in collaboratively and checked against an OHP, or later against a book illustration.

* Photographs

— Photocopy photographs and 35 mm slides. Use them in the session and/or for later reference.

* Questionnaires

— Construct some short, not-too-serious items.
— Use multiple choice; true/false; diagram labelling; *What's the question to which this is the answer?* etc.
— Produce a 'split half' and allow partners to test each other.
— Ask pairs to write one question + its correct answer on a card, collect them in, then read out appropriate ones as a test for the whole group. Allow them to work in pairs ... and get one right!

* Collation

— Copy (and bind with a cover and index) each small group's solution to completed tasks and return a set to everyone.
— Reduce A4 to A5 and print as a centre-staple booklet.
— Agree how they are to be distributed.

* Blank cards

— Have blank record cards for the tasks you may spontaneously decide to do in the session. Give them out as needed but include one in any 'enveloped sets' you use.

8 **Assessment and Review**: Assessing the extent to which individuals are learning during a session (and what they have learnt by the end) is not easy with a large group. Finding out how they are reacting to the session and what they thought about it at the end is less problematic. Judgement may have to rely as much upon impression as on objective evidence of individual change. Where you meet individuals and small groups subsequently (in tutorials, seminars or workshops), or where they are involved in some formal assessment procedure, you will be able to follow up learning outcomes. Otherwise, you could employ some of the following:

* Collaborative

    – Ask individuals to review their notes on what has been covered so far (say after 20 or so minutes), then collaboratively write a brief *resumé* from memory.
    – Alternatively, suggest they explain some or all of the main points to a partner and/or note down (with a partner's help) what else they need to do/read/practice to master the topic.
    – Monitor how they have done and ask what you can explain further.

* Questioning
    – Avoid asking direct questions of identified individuals; questions addressed generally may be more acceptable but still may not elicit much response.
    – Ask questions — problem solving, factual, critical opinion, etc, — where people individually note down their answer on paper. Alternatively, ask them to work together and offer you an answer, or they check out each other's answer.
    – Monitor how they have done and confirm the correct version. Elaborate, or give further examples of your own opinion as required.
    – Asking *Do you understand* usually elicits uncertain 'yesses'. Ask obliquely: *Are you happy ... should I go over anything once again to be sure ... can I pick up any points for clarification?*

* Observation

    – Watch the audience for 'cues and clues'. Identify whether people are attentive, enthusiastic, alert to nuances, responsive to requests, taking notes ... chatting, yawning or asleep.

* 'Tests'

- Avoid anything too formal or serious; the main purpose for learners is to find out for themselves what they know. Avoid competition; results from collaborative work will tell you (and each individual) nearly as much.
- Select informal techniques but construct worthwhile items — label a diagram; draw a flow chart; re-order the items; note down 'x' important features of 'y', etc.
- Strike a balance between being too threatening and too childish.
- Do not show up those who have not done too well.

* Evaluation

- Employ a short and simple evaluation which is completed on the spot (collaboratively) and returned.
- Include an item: *What are you taking away with you of value?*
- Organise the time so that the evaluation is completed at least 5 minutes before the end so that you can finish with a 'punchy' finale.
- Be on hand as they leave to 'earwig' comments; ask people informally what use the session was to them.

KEY POINTS

❑ **Use a range of strategies and techniques to provide both variety and interest.**

❑ **Look for ways in which people can actively participate more and you can talk less.**

... and finally ...

Learning remains the responsibility of the adult learner; as teachers we cannot learn for our students. We can, however, strive to provide sound and accessible learning opportunities for them by thoughtful planning and preparation, by well-run sessions and by careful evaluation of the whole process. Successful outcomes say something about the quality of our shared efforts: *adult teaching and adult learning.*

26   Further reading

Adults Learning   *(NIACE, National Institute of Adult and Continuing Education 19B, De Montfort Street, Leciester LE1 7GE).* The **monthly journal** of NIACE; it includes a variety of articles and up-to-date information on current developments in practice and policy plus news of forthcoming events. Worth subscribing to.

Studies in the Education of Adults *(NIACE).* The **biannual journal** of studies in all post-initial education and training. Academic. Look at library copies when you feel strong.

Resources for Teachers of Adults
John Cummins and others, (NIACE) 1987. A handbook of practical advice on audio-visual aids and educational technology. Useful. Does not include Marler-Haley 'velcro' display.

Teaching in Further Education
LB Curzon, Holt Education, 3rd edition 1985. Sound and well-revised text directed at FE teachers (at C&G 7307/5 level).

Education for Adults
·from HMI "Education Observed" series, HMSO 1991. Provides a brief review of adult education based on HMI reports. Read a library copy.

Teaching Skills in Further and Adult Education
David Minton, Macmillan and City and Guilds, 1991. Concentrates on FE rather than AE and slanted towards the C&G 7307/5 Teachers' Certificate Course. Rather patchy.

Tutors Tool-kit
Rosemary Napper and Diana Batchelor, NEC 1989 (see below). Described as an open learning resource for first-time tutors. Good if you like working through activities given in a text. Covers similar ground to *Adult Learning, Adult Teaching.* Expensive**.**

NEC publications
National Extension College, 18 Brooklands Avenue, Cambridge. Publishes a number of learning resources and training materials — especially useful on teacher development, counselling and guidance, open learning, basic education, ESOL, etc. All rather pricey but do get their brochure and see for yourself.

Teaching Adults

Alan Rogers, Open University Press, 1989. Thorough treatment though idiosyncratic views. Particularly concerned with AE rather than FE. Valuable 'advanced companion' to *Adult Learning, Adult Teaching.*

Adult Learning

Jennifer Rogers, Open University Press (3rd Edition) 1990. One of the first — very readable and practical. Well worth buying as a starter text.

Adult Education

Michael Stephens, Cassell, 1990. Gives an accessible account of the current world of adult education. Personal at times but a helpful introduction to the field.

Other texts include:

Evaluation in Adult and Further Education, *Judith Edwards, WEA, 1991*

The Black Perspective in Adult Education, *FEU, 1989*

Adult and Continuing Education, *Peter Jarvis, Croom Helm, 1983*

Access to Education for Non-participative Adults, *Veronica McGivney, NIACE, 1991*

Women Learning: Ideas, Approaches & ... Support, *Replan/NIACE, 1991*

Learning and Leisure, *Naomi Sargeant, NIACE, 1991*

Adults with Learning Difficulties, *Jeannie Sutcliffe, NIACE, 1990*

The **'53 interesting ways to ...'** series, *Technical Educ. Services Ltd.*

The Psychology of Adult Learning, *Mark Tennant, Routledge, 1989*

Teaching and Learning in FE, *L Walklin, Stanley Thomas, 1990*

27   Staff development opportunities

Staff development and training opportunities for part-time and full-time teachers of adults are available in most areas of the UK. They range from individual support networks, day, weekend and evening workshops on general and subject specific themes to longer formal courses. Such courses include the regional 'ACSET' Stage 1 (and occasionally Stage 2) course for teachers of adults; the City and Guilds 7307/5 course, Stages 1 and 2; the Certificate in Education (FE) and, more rarely, the Certificate in Education (AE). For further details, contact your centre head or head of department; the LEA adult education/community education staff; the LEA INSET training officer; the LEA Adult Guidance Service; the local college of FE City and Guilds 7307/5 course tutor; the local HE institution. A number of private firms and individuals working as consultants offer short courses directed particularly at business personnel, though they are usually very expensive.

The Department of Adult Education at the University of Nottingham provides a range of workshops and short courses as 'in-house' staff development provision for any agency or institution whose staff are concerned with teaching and working with adults. John Daines and Brian Graham, who run these courses, can be contacted at the University to discuss ways in which the needs of potential participants can best be met.

There is also a huge range of subject-specialist/professional bodies who provide adult education in a variety of guises and a number provide training for their teachers. These include the Keep Fit Association, St John Ambulance, Royal Yacht Association, the Quilters Guild, the Workers' Educational Association, the Women's Institute, and many more. There are several subject-based teacher training courses offered by, for example, the Royal Society of Arts in conjunction with other bodies such as the YMCA and the Health Education Authority.

Advanced academic study of adult and continuing education is available through many University Departments of Adult and Continuing Education (including the Open University) and some Colleges of Higher Education.

There are four organisations of interest to teachers of adults:

NIACE: *National Institute of Adult and Continuing Education, 19B De Montfort Street, Leicester, LE1 7GE (0533 551451)* The major representative body of all adult and continuing education.

CEDC: *Community Education Development Centre, Lyng Hall, Blackberry Lane, Coventry, CV2 3JS (0203 638660)* Offers courses and resources. Publishes "Network" monthly.

ECA: *Educational Centres Association, Chequer Court, Chequer Street, London EC1Y 8PL (071 251 4158)* Has joint student, staff, and Centre membership. Focuses on liberal adult education.

NATFHE: *National Association of Teachers in Further and Higher Education, 27 Britannia Street, London, WC1X 9JP (071 837 3636)* A trade union for all post-16, full-time and part-time teachers.